SCHOLASTIC

◆

Classroom Discussion

Strategies for Engaging *All* Students, Building Higher-Level Thinking Skills, and Strengthening Reading and Writing Across the Curriculum

BY DIXIE LEE SPIEGEL

New York • Toronto • London • Auckland • Sydney
Mexico City • New Delhi • Hong Kong • Buenos Aires

Teaching *Resources*

◆

Dedication

I dedicate this book to my family and my friends inside and outside of the
School of Education at the University of North Carolina at Chapel Hill,
who have shown such love and care for me over the years.

Credit, pages 51–52: Lyrics from *Old Folks* are from *Jacques Brel Is Alive and Well and Living in Paris*. English lyrics by Eric Blau and Mort Shuman based on Jacques Brel's lyrics and commentary, published by Mort Shuman Songs, Warner Brothers Publications.

Cover design by James Sarfati
Interior design by LDL Designs
Cover photo: The Image Bank/Getty Images
Interior photos: Page 8: © Majlah Feanny/Corbis; Page 9: © Brendan Byrne/DigitalVision;
Page 21: © Gabe Palmer/Corbis; Page 57: © Dan Lamont/Corbis; Page 85: © Gabe Palmer/Corbis;
Page 101: © Jim Sugar/Corbis; Page 109: © Majlah Feanny/Corbis

ISBN 0-439-56757-2
Copyright © 2005 by Dixie Lee Spiegel
All rights reserved. Published by Scholastic Inc.
Printed in the U.S.A.

3 4 5 6 7 8 9 10 23   11 10 09 08 07

Contents

Acknowledgments 5

Foreword by P. David Pearson 6

Introduction 8

Chapter One: 9
Classroom Discussion: What It Is and Why It Is Important

The Characteristics of True Discussion 10

The Benefits of True Discussion 14

Final Thought 20

Chapter Two: 21
Enhancing Learning in the Content Areas Through Discussion

Why Use Discussion Across the Curriculum? 22

How Can Discussion Be Used for Preparation and Follow-Up? 26

What Time Factors Must Be Considered for Discussion to Work? 35

Discussion in Individual Content Areas 42

Final Thought 56

Chapter Three: 57
Preparing for Discussion: Setting Up for Success

Preparing the Classroom Climate for Discussion 58

Making Decisions About Groups and Grouping 59

Selecting Questions for Discussion 77

Ensuring Students Come to Small-Group Discussions Well Informed 80

Final Thought 84

Chapter Four: 85
Facilitating Discussion: Scaffolding Instruction to Help Students Take Off

Tap Students' Understandings: Developing Ownership of the Discussion 87

Invite Participation: Ensuring All Students Have a Voice 89

Orchestrate the Discussion: Gaining and Maintaining Momentum 92

Seek Clarification: Building Understanding 95

Final Thought 100

Chapter Five: **101**

Following Up Discussion: Keeping the Thinking Alive

Mini-Lessons 102

Reflection Journals 104

Thinking Charts 108

Final Thought 108

Chapter Six: **109**

Assessing Discussion: Determining if Your Efforts Are Paying Off

Develop an Overall Plan for Assessment 110

Four Important Aspects of Assessing Discussion 117

Record Keeping 127

Final Thought 128

Appendices **129**

Discussion Web 130

Listening In on Discussion Form 131

Confidence Rating Form 132

Vocabulary Expectations Chart 133

Planning Chart for Whole-Class Discussion 134

Discussion Planning Sheet 135

Continuing Thinking After Discussion 136

Analyzing Reflection Journal Entries 137

Tracking My Thinking 138

Rubric: Postdiscussion Journal Entries 139

Determining if You Have a Discussion Curriculum in Place 140

Discussion Goals Checklist 141

Plan for a Teacher Workshop Based on This Book 143

References **152**

Children's Literature Cited 152

Professional Literature Cited 153

Index **157**

Acknowledgments

I would like to thank my colleagues at the University of North Carolina at Chapel Hill for their guidance: Susan Friel (mathematics), Xue Lan Rong (social studies), Beth Shaw McGuire (the arts), Alan Tom (social studies), and William Veal (science). Thanks also to my middle school consultants, Elena and Nina Versenyi. Thanks to P. David Pearson for his insightful foreword, which sets the context for the book as a tool for teachers of all subjects in a democratic society. And special thanks go to the editor of every writer's dreams, Ray Coutu, who gently nudged me when my writing didn't make sense (oh, how tactfully he could say, "Huh?"), edited out the redundancies in my language, and was patient when deadlines didn't always get met. Thanks, Ray. You are the best.

Foreword

by P. David Pearson,
University of California, Berkeley

Dixie Lee Spiegel has done us all (teachers, future teachers, teacher educators, and staff developers) a big favor—gathering in one place our collective knowledge, wisdom, and good advice about how to promote the sort of talk about text that creates access to academic success and personal insight for students. She helps us understand that discussion is a tool that teachers and students can and should use to enhance their comprehension of text. She gives us enough theory and research background so that we understand that reading is as much a social act as it is an individual act—that when students share their personal understandings with peers, they benefit as individuals, extending and enriching the personal understandings they build when reading on their own.

As adults we should know this because we do it every day—in discussing movies, books, television shows, and even news events. We rely on others to test and shape our understandings:

"So, whaddya think about that movie?"

"I liked it."

"I didn't."

"Great characters, but a thin plot."

"Not as good as his last one."

"At least it was funny."

"That's something, I suppose."

Spiegel also reminds us that it is during rich discussions, which can take place not only in literature classes but also in history, science, and even math classes, that students gain another important competency—engaging in academic discourse. Much of what we label academic discourse is really learning the language that is embodied in our academic texts and the ways in which we talk about those texts. Whether we call it literary criticism, scientific inquiry, mathematical problem-solving, or historical reasoning, the name of the game is learning how to make claims (beliefs, opinions, or assertions about how the world works) and use evidence (sometimes from written texts, sometimes from experience, and other times from the conversations we hold about text) to support those claims. Much of Spiegel's advice focuses on how teachers can encourage students to use texts for the evidence they need to warrant their interpretations. She points out discussions serve a dual function: *(a)* to enrich our understandings of text and, equally important, *(b)* to provide a place in which we can learn the skills of participating in a community—a worthy educational goal in its own right because it moves students beyond academic discourse to democratic discourse, which is the backbone of any democracy.

Another admirable feature of this wonderful book is its even-handedness across subject matters. Truth be told, most authors who write about discussion often limit their deliberations to reading and literature classes, leaving discussion about the information genres to the whims of content area teachers' experience (or lack of experience). This is unfortunate, because students may infer that the interpretive and critical eye that we encourage them to use when reading literary texts should remain in English class and that they should defer to "veridical" reading, in which they ferret out the truth embodied in informational pieces, in content area classes. Ultimately, discouraging critical reading of expository text is counterproductive, for it sells our democracy short by assuming that we should always believe what we read, unless it is in a piece of fiction. A free and open society assumes a critical readership—one that can smell a rat and tell the difference between a valid argument and propaganda. Fortunately for us, Spiegel travels down a different road, one on which we encounter lots of examples to help us guide critical reading of all sorts of texts, including the informational genres of social studies, science, and mathematics. In fact, Spiegel goes a step further by treating literature as a subject on par with science and social studies. This is a perspective that I have long advocated because it casts reading, writing, and speaking as a set of basic skills, just like learning, that can be applied to a wide range of texts and contexts, not just literature.

Spiegel asserts that good talk about text won't happen magically just by giving kids good things to read or asking them open questions about text. She understands what all of us who have spent time in classrooms know—that extensive modeling, guided practice of strategies for developing good answers and good questions, and lots of opportunities to "do it on your own" in a range of groupings (large, small, homogeneous, heterogeneous) without the teacher looking over your shoulder are necessary for students to become independent critical readers who can hold their own in a discussion about a text.

This book provides the right balance of theoretical grounding, explanation of the rationale and research behind various practices, and rich elaborations of the practices themselves that a teacher needs to achieve a dramatic turnaround—or a slight shift in what she's already doing. Teachers who take advantage of this opportunity will find themselves in classrooms with more vibrant, more engaged, and more critical readers. And that is a very good place to be. Happy reading (and talking)!

Introduction

These days, teachers are being held accountable for student performance more than ever before. As a result, developing discussion skills and encouraging discussion often take a backseat to teaching the mandated curriculum or preparing students for standardized tests. Some teachers even discourage talk, resulting in students who are "talk-deprived" and view classroom discussion as an activity only to be carried on surreptitiously (Alvermann et al., 1996). Or students may come to view discussion as a waste of time, leading them to ask that age-old, annoying question, "Will it be on the test?" In my work with teachers, I've found that discussion in classrooms is often hurried, superficial, ineffective, and  sometimes even completely absent. This is a tragedy, considering the power that discussion brings to the classroom.

This book is designed to help you use discussion as a tool for building student engagement and learning in social studies, science, mathematics, health, and the arts, not just in language arts. It will help you prepare students for meaningful discussions, guide them as they discuss, and provide them with follow-up activities to solidify and extend new understandings. In Chapter 1, I describe the characteristics and benefits of true discussion. Chapter 2 focuses on the place of discussion in the curriculum and how discussion can be used to enhance student learning in all subjects. Chapter 3 centers around creating a classroom climate that fosters discussion and making decisions about grouping and groups. In Chapter 4, I show how teacher scaffolding prepares students to run small-group discussions and, in Chapter 5, I suggest ways to encourage students to continue thinking about what they have discussed long after the discussion has ended. In the final chapter, I provide guidelines and a framework for assessment, along with sample assessment plans. Throughout the book, I sprinkle Listening In activities that give pointers on what to look for and teach when you "eavesdrop" on discussions in your classroom. I also provide Discussion Stifler boxes throughout, listing surefire ways to kill a discussion. In other words, these are ways *not* to teach! The appendix contains handy, reproducible forms for planning, carrying out, and assessing discussions.

I hope this book helps you use classroom discussion to make learning rich, rigorous, and satisfying for all your students.

Chapter One

Classroom Discussion: What It Is and Why It Is Important

Discussion is an important tool of learning. It engages students, broadens their perspectives, and promotes meaning-making, decision-making, and higher-level thinking. Discussion is difficult, even for adults. We converse, we share, we argue, we report, and we think we have discussed. But true discussion is purposeful interchange of ideas through which meaning has the possibility of being revised and extended. In this chapter, I delve into the characteristics and benefits of true discussion to give you the knowledge and confidence you need to carry it out daily in your classroom.

The Characteristics of True Discussion

According to Martin Nystrand and Adam Gamoran (1993), discussion is "the thoughtful and sustained examination of a given topic over a period of time involving substantial contributions and reflections by [all participants]" (p. 99). This is a good definition, but true discussion has many other important characteristics, which I describe in this section.

Discussion Is Open-Ended

Discussion needs to be focused on a topic; otherwise it is just free-flowing conversation. However, it should not be viewed as a closed task, the goal being to arrive at one right answer to one question. By its very nature, discussion should shift back and forth across topics and subtopics, as participants exchange different perspectives. In a truly open-ended discussion, participants are tentative, moving forward with one idea, retreating, changing direction, exploring a new topic, abandoning that topic, and so on. They must be receptive to new ideas, amenable to reconsidering their own ideas, and agreeable to taking side trips as the topic expands. Their discussion has a spontaneous quality, and as a result, it is complex. If you were to chart the flow of a true discussion, it would probably show more than one main topic, several subtopics, some blind alleys, and many arrows connecting participants' comments.

EXAMPLE OF TALK AROUND A CLOSED TASK

TEACHER: What are the first-aid steps to follow for CPR?

RALPH: You press the chest right below …

TEACHER: Is that the first thing you do?

BIANCA: No. First, you check that their airway is clear, that they can get air into their lungs.

TEACHER: Okay. There's no point in doing chest compressions unless air can get in. What do you do next?

PAUL: You tilt their head back and pinch their nose shut.

TEACHER: Why do you pinch the nose shut?

RASHAD: So that when you breathe into their mouth, the air goes into the lungs and not just right out the nose.

BIANCA: And then you breathe into the mouth, as hard as you can.

RALPH: No, no. Not hard. Just three quick puffs. Then you do the chest compressions.

This is an example of single-minded talk, with the teacher prompting students to provide a set of correct answers about administering CPR. There's little interaction among the students and no spontaneity. Students aren't receptive to the ideas of others because their purpose is to provide correct answers, not explore different ideas. This talk is an example of the IRE pattern (Nystrand & Gamoran, 1991):

I = The teacher *interrogates*.   R = The students *respond*.   E = The teacher *evaluates* the responses.

IRE can be useful when you want to teach students a body of knowledge and assess what they have learned. In fact, the choice of IRE for the example above is appropriate because the teacher wants to know if the students have learned the specific steps in administering CPR. So IRE has its place in the classroom, but it is not discussion.

Compare the last example to the next one, which comes from Jeni Day's fifth-grade class. Notice how the girls tentatively explore why they like or don't like the book *The Pinballs* by Betsy Byars (1993). The discussion leads them to clarify their thoughts. Notice, too, how the group spontaneously shifts back and forth across subtopics.

EXAMPLE OF AN OPEN-ENDED DISCUSSION

KATE: Our prompt was "Do you like this book better than *Cracker Jackson* [1996]?"

ANNA: I didn't like this book better than *Cracker Jackson*. It's not as exciting, because I think it's plain stupid.

KATE: Did anyone enjoy the book?

TANYA: It's not interesting. It's boring. I don't know why; it just is.

KATE: Do you like this book better than *Cracker Jackson*?

SHEREICE: I love it.

KATE: Why?

SHEREICE: I don't know why.

KATHY: We might not be far enough into the book yet. We've already finished *Cracker Jackson,* and it is in the last half of the book that the more exciting parts happened, and right now we're just in the middle of this one. So I don't think we're far enough into this book to decide. I think I might end up liking *Pinballs* better because it's just so emotional. It gives you so many feelings about how it would be to live with a foster mother and have your parents be drunk and run over your legs.

[The students briefly discuss the author of the two books.]

ANNA: This book isn't as good, because it's boring.

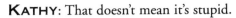

KATHY: That doesn't mean it's stupid.

ANNA: There's no action. And it takes them so long to see that they can take care of their own lives. It's just kind of stupid.

[The students move to the subtopic of how much control the characters have over their lives.]

KATE: Well, they're kids. And they don't exactly come from a great home. And they might not have known they can take care of their own lives.

ANNA: They can control their own lives.

KATE: Well, this girl Carlie, she was hit by a frying pan, by her stepfather, wasn't it? And then she hit him back, but then she went unconscious. I don't think you can take care of yourself when you're unconscious. It's a little hard!

[The students continue discussing this subtopic for a while, then move on to why Carlie is so hateful. They try to figure out how old Carlie is, and then return to the subtopic of having control in life.]

KATE: Is there anything you want to say?

KATHY: You mean about taking control of your life?

ANNA: They can make their own decisions. Anybody could.

TANYA: That's all I do.

KATE: I know, but what if they let them take control of their lives right now and let them make their own decisions? What if they make the wrong decision? They still need a little help.

KATHY: You can be really young and make decisions, but that doesn't make them the right ones.

ANNA: There is no right decision.

KATE: But some are better than others.

[The students continue discussing this subtopic and then move on to a procedural discussion about how far in the book to read for the next week.]

Discussion Is Recursive, Not Linear

When describing her work on classroom discussion with seventh graders, Carol Gilles (1993) says, "Few topics emerged neatly. Students often moved quickly from one topic to another and returned to those they considered important. This dynamic, circular movement I've labeled 'cycles of meaning' " (p. 206). You can see these cycles in the open-ended discussion example above. The girls begin with a discussion about which of the two books they prefer, touch on the fact that both books were written by the same author, return to discussing why they liked one book better than the other, and then go on to discuss the amount of control the characters have over their lives, focusing on Carlie. This leads to a brief exploration of Carlie's hateful personality and her age. The group then returns to the issue of control, an issue of great interest to the participants, which for most is made clear for the first time by the discussion.

This circularity, these cycles of meaning, allows discussion to be self-sustaining. The participants naturally return to topics and subtopics of interest, interjecting new ideas, reacting to the ideas of others, and revising their own ideas accordingly. If uninterrupted, the discussion continues until the participants have explored the topic to their satisfaction.

Discussion Is Collaborative and Constructive

If talk is not collaborative, then it is not truly a discussion. It is reporting, with each participant presenting ideas without reference to the ideas of others. Discussion involves sharing ideas, listening to and taking into consideration the perspectives of others, and working together to build meaning. This kind of collaboration allows the group to construct meaning from the ideas of all participants. For this to happen, though, participants have to listen and respond. If one participant dominates, the discussion becomes a lecture. Note in the example below how Jeni Day's fifth graders negotiate back and forth to construct meaning. They may not end up in agreement, but each participant hears and responds to the perspectives of others.

TANYA: When I play games and things, the other people are not all girls. There are some boys and girls. The boys think that us girls can't do as much as they do. They think that they are a whole lot better than us.

KATE: Especially in sports.

KATHY: I'm not going to name names, but there are some boys in this classroom that just think the girls are not as good as them, but we are better.

BRUCE: That's not always true.

KATE: Yes, it is.

BRUCE: Sometimes it's true.

KATE: Well, better than some boys.

BRUCE: I'm not good at basketball.

KATE: I'm better than Gregory.

TANYA: I think if boys would give us girls more chances to do things, then maybe they'll see the boys aren't everything.

> ## LISTENING IN
>
> Tape-record several interactions in your classroom, listen to the tapes, and categorize each interaction as "discussion" or "not discussion." From there, develop a checklist you can use to identify true discussion on an ongoing basis. (See Appendix 12 for an example of a checklist.)

The Benefits of True Discussion

Discussion allows students to explore and understand the curriculum. Through the social interaction of discussion, students make meaning. Discussion can lead to a richer, deeper understanding of the curriculum and can promote higher-level thinking. It also increases engagement and ownership of ideas and invites participation of all students, regardless of their literacy level. I explore each of these benefits in this section.

Discussion Allows Students to Make Meaning Through Social Interaction

Although we can construct meaning all by ourselves, we enrich and revise individually constructed meanings through social interaction, through exposure to the ideas of others (Bloome & Green, 1992). Without social interaction, there is little reason to revisit, rethink, or refine ideas. Janice Almasi (1995) argues that conceptual change comes about from realizing that others do not agree with us.

In a true discussion, our ideas are filtered through the ideas of others. One person puts forth an idea, and others respond by agreeing or disagreeing or by modifying, refuting, or extending that idea. The initial speaker then considers those responses and may repeat, modify, or extend the original idea. The ideas of others serve as a filter through which ideas pass, and in the process, meaning changes.

In fact, through social interaction, our thinking becomes clearer and more explicit (Gilles, 1993). This comes about in two ways:

> "We need each other. We need each other to find out what we know, how we know, what we think, and how we think."
>
> – Linda Sheppard

◆ **By gathering our thoughts in preparation for expressing them.** The most effective discussions occur when participants take time beforehand to think about what they will say and how they will say it. If ideas are not expressed clearly, they may be dismissed without response or misinterpreted. To avoid this, participants should come to the discussion prepared.

◆ **By considering the responses to our ideas.** As others challenge, extend, and even agree with an idea, participants may be forced to a deeper level of thought in order to respond by either supporting or modifying their original position. Speakers may need to move beyond a relatively superficial idea to an awareness of how they arrived at their idea in the first place. As participants evaluate and accommodate the responses of others, their thinking is defined and refined (Chase & Hynd, 1987, p. 533).

Students also gain an appreciation of multiple perspectives during discussion, which can lead them to reflect on and possibly revise their ideas. But, without true consideration of others' perspectives, there is no discussion, only the serial presentation of ideas. Janice Almasi (1995) points out that the conflicting ideas that may arise from multiple perspectives are valuable because they encourage students to think about other interpretations and not just rely on their own isolated ideas.

Ralph Peterson and Maryann Eeds (1990) provide two simple rules for effective discussion related to Almasi's belief: "The first is to respect the interpretation of others and help in their development whenever possible. It is not necessary to adopt other interpretations, but everyone is obliged to listen to them and give them full consideration. The second rule is that participants, teachers and students, must not enter dialogue with an agenda in mind" (p. 22). Participants must move beyond their own ideas, embrace the ideas of others, and accept the fact that, although different, these ideas may be as valid as their own. They must learn that their ideas can be strengthened and made better by considering others' points of view. They must learn, too, that sometimes their ideas aren't valid while another person's idea simply makes better sense.

Discussion Leads to Richer, Deeper Meaning

True discussion is not summarizing ideas or searching for "correct" answers but genuinely collaborating in a way that leads to a deeper or entirely new meaning. It is a process of coproducing meaning (Peterson & Eeds, 1990) by sharing the different interpretations that our varying sets of background knowledge, inferences, and interests invariably create. Participants fill in gaps for each other. Susan McMahon (1994) describes it well: Fifth graders in the book clubs she observed could "coconstruct an explanation that no individual student understood alone, but together they could explain" (p. 113).

Discussion is an ideal mechanism for promoting rethinking and, therefore, the revision of meaning. Carol Gilles (1993) uses "cycles of meaning" to describe the revision of meaning within a discussion. But we can extend this idea to think of cycles of meaning *before*, *during*, and *after* discussion.

CYCLES OF MEANING

Cycle 1	Cycle 2	Cycle 3
Before Discussion: Students activate existing meanings and bring them to the discussion.	**During Discussion:** Students develop new meanings and clarify and alter existing meanings.	**After Discussion:** Students continue to reflect on and revise meanings.

In the first cycle of meaning, students develop schemas about a topic, creating mental networks of information about what they know. The schemas may be extensive or sparse; they may be accurate or flawed; they may be organized or disorganized. Students may or may not be aware of what they know, of what meaning they have made. Clearly, the more aware students are of what they know, the better prepared they are for discussion.

Cycle One: What David Brings to the Discussion

1. whats on sale in the cafeteria
2. Which teachers we have !!
3. if we can go off campus to Burger King next door
4. how much homework we have
5. the dress code

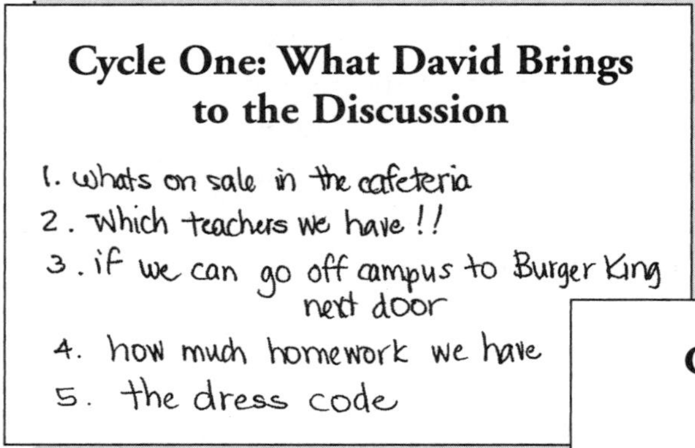

FIGURE 1-1: What David considers in Cycle 1, before the discussion.

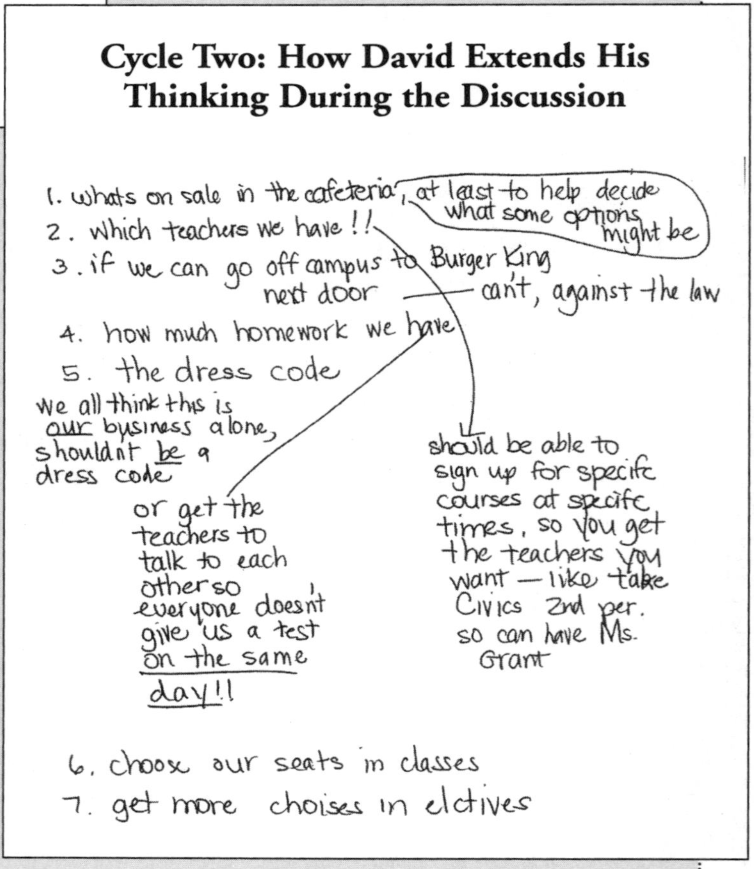

Let's follow the cycles of meaning of one middle school student, David, as he and his peers ponder the question "What kinds of decisions should students be able to make?"

Cycle Two: How David Extends His Thinking During the Discussion

1. whats on sale in the cafeteria — at least to help decide what some options might be
2. Which teachers we have !!
3. if we can go off campus to Burger King next door — can't, against the law
4. how much homework we have
5. the dress code

We all think this is our business alone, shouldn't be a dress code

or get the teachers to talk to each other so everyone doesn't give us a test on the same day!!

should be able to sign up for specific courses at specific times, so you get the teachers you want — like take Civics 2nd per. so can have Ms. Grant

6. choose our seats in classes
7. get more choises in elctives

FIGURE 1-2: During the discussion with his peers, David narrows his view on decision 1, clarifies what he means for 2, eliminates 3 because of new information, refines 4, confirms 5, and adds 6 and 7.

In the second cycle, meanings are developed, clarified, and altered. This is not to say that meaning must change during discussion, but meaning must always have the potential to change. Participants must come to the group understanding that the purpose of discussion is to broaden their perspectives, clarify their ideas, and give them new information. Bahktin (1981) describes true discussion as "a constant interaction between meanings, all of which have the potential of conditioning others" (p. 426).

During Cycle 2, new and richer meaning may be created as participants see through the lenses of others in the group, scaffold their understandings (Leal, 1993), and join in collaborative efforts to forge new meanings. Almasi (1995) points out the importance of sociocognitive conflict for the continued development of meaning, whereby participants are forced to consider interpretations other than their own. Figure 1-2 demonstrates how David extends his thinking during the discussion.

Cycle Three: What David Learns as a Result of the Discussion

1. whats on sale in the cafeteria, at least to help decide what some options might be
2. Which teachers we have !!
3. if we can go off campus to Burger King next door — can't, against the law
4. how much homework we have
5. the dress code
   We all think this is our business alone, shouldn't be a dress code
   #5 but we need to ban racist cloths
   #1 maybe we could vote on vending machines and what is in them
   should be able to sign up for specific courses at specific times, so you get the teachers you want — like take Civics 2nd per. so can have Ms. Grant
   or get the teachers to talk to each other so everyone doesn't give us a test on the same day!! maybe we could get assigned homework by day — Civics (Mon.), Math (Tues)
6. choose our seats in classes. But what if 2 of us want the same seat? How often can we change?
7. get more choises in elctives like a movie criticsm course, jazz, ti kwondoo
8. who the dj is at the Spring Fling

FIGURE 1-3: In Cycle 3, after the discussion, David continues to expand and refine his ideas. With decisions 1, 4, and 7 his ideas became more sophisticated and specific. He maintained his belief in 2 and found a qualifier for 5. He began to recognize some problems with 6 and added another potential decision, 8, an idea that is less grandiose than those on his original list and reflects his increasing understanding of the issues of choice.

Meaning is developed, clarified, and altered not only by hearing the ideas of others but also by expressing one's own meaning. Participating in a discussion leads students to express their ideas clearly and be explicit in their own thinking. Their metacognition (their understanding about what they know) may be heightened as they struggle to explain to others what they mean. Discussion can also be what I. A. Richards (1942) called an "audit of meaning" (p. 240), a mechanism for checking the validity and fullness of one's ideas. Richards was referring to writing, but discussion can serve the same purpose.

> "When one child expresses his or her personal prior knowledge, the prior knowledge of other participants is activated. These shared thoughts stimulate further ideas from others in the group and result in the collaborative construction of meaning for all. In essence, shared prior knowledge about a particular topic or text becomes 'corporate knowledge' and part of the discussion group's textual understanding."
> – Dorothy Leal

If discussion is effective, individuals will come away with new perspectives and perhaps the understanding that ideas can be complex. But hopefully this is not the end of meaning-making. After a discussion, students need time to reflect, consolidate, and refine their new understandings, which is what the third cycle is all about. Think of Cycle 3 as a fine stew: an amalgam of ideas simmering over time, blending to provide richness and flavor. You can see the results of this simmering in Figure 1-3.

When working alone, students often read (or listen to or view) the assignment and call it "done" all too quickly, without any real thought about what they have just taken in. Discussion forces students to explore ideas more fully, to clarify their own thinking, to hear other interpretations, and to review what they have read or thought. It gives them the time (and requires them) to think and rethink. Therefore, it leads to richer, deeper understanding.

Discussion Promotes Higher-Level Thinking

True discussion is by definition open-ended: It leads to no one correct answer and offers no single way to arrive at possible answers. Julianne Turner and Scott Paris (1995) describe open tasks as problems to be solved, and because they "are more cognitively complex than closed tasks, they require students to think strategically" (p. 667). They explain that this strategic, or higher-level, thinking includes goal setting, choosing and organizing information, and assessing outcomes, and it is critical to successful discussion.

Joyce Many and Donna Wiseman (1992) found evidence of higher-level thinking in third-grade students who discussed picture books they had read, and the most sophisticated thinking came from the group with the most open-ended tasks. Each class was randomly formed into three groups. One group met to discuss how the students would feel if they were in the situation portrayed in the story, an open-ended task. Another group discussed character analysis and problems and solutions, a relatively closed task that yielded fewer divergent answers. The third group, the control group, did not discuss the story after reading it. All the students responded to this prompt: "Write anything you want about the story you just read." The students who had discussed their feelings about the story wrote responses that were more elaborate than the others'; they formed judgments, described images they had of the events, and made associations between the story and real life. Their responses were quite sophisticated and showed a great deal of involvement in the world of the story. For example, some children described similarities between real people and characters in the story. By contrast, students who did not discuss the story or tackled the relatively closed questions tended simply to retell the story events in their written responses.

Margaret Anzul (1993) found that book discussion allowed fifth- and sixth-grade students to lift their thinking to a higher level, much more so than if the teacher had lectured them about what they should be looking for. She reports that students became quite adept at describing the thinking that led to their interpretations.

Another kind of higher-level thinking that discussion promotes is metacognition, which, as mentioned earlier, is knowing about your own knowing: knowing if you know, if you don't know, and how to "fix" your knowing. Gilles (1993) points out that when individuals are building meaning by themselves, they don't notice the process. They aren't aware of the way their thinking functions and how meaning evolves from there. But when individuals are in a group, they are forced to think about their own thinking, to explain themselves, to notice that someone has a different idea, and to consider whether they want to modify their own ideas based on those of others. Under these circumstances, individuals think about their thinking. They begin to notice flaws in their own logic and develop strategies for avoiding ineffective ways of thinking.

Discussion Increases Engagement with and Ownership of Ideas

John Guthrie and his colleagues (1996) define engagement as "the integration of motivations and strategies" (p. 306). If readers (or listeners or viewers) are engaged, they will be more likely to use strategies to understand, to explore problems, and to move toward solutions. Thus, engagement is involvement.

Engagement is critical because it has been shown to lead to deeper processing of ideas and increased learning. Many of the characteristics and benefits of discussion are directly related to engagement, including maintaining open-endedness, building on responses rather than evaluating them, controlling one's own learning, and collaborating (Nystrand & Gamoran, 1991; Turner & Paris, 1995). An interesting and consistent finding about discussion is that students often "ignore" teachers once they are engaged (Alvermann et al., 1996). A teacher's effort to interject or refocus a topic may not be acknowledged because the group is committed to its own exploration. The participants have achieved ownership of the discussion and the ideas and are not about to give up the floor to the teacher!

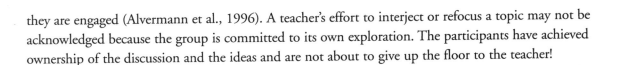

ENGAGEMENT ➡➡ DEEPER PROCESSING ➡➡ INCREASED LEARNING

Students who are engaged in a topic are more likely to explore that topic longer and more deeply than students who are not. As a result, they learn more about the topic.

Discussion Allows Participation of All Students, Regardless of Literacy Level

Discussion is inclusive. If we find ways for all students to come to a discussion with access to the ideas, with something to discuss, then all students can participate. That "if," of course, is tricky because students come to us at a variety of literacy levels. For students who are unable to read an assigned text, less challenging texts on the same topic may be provided (and may present information not contained in the assigned text) or the information may be made accessible through video or audio sources. Once students have the ideas, they are freed from the boundaries of their literacy levels and the playing field for discussion is somewhat leveled.

In essence, I'm saying that discussion is a chance for all students to have a voice. Too often and for a variety of reasons, students are silenced, but with a little preparation, every student can join the discussion. Then they can express their views, learn from each other, and be seen as resources by their classmates.

Final Thought

Discussion should be considered not a frill but rather an essential component of the curriculum, just like reading and writing. It is a tool that leads to deeper understanding, active participation, and higher-level thinking. In the next chapter, you will learn more about how discussion can enhance learning throughout the curriculum.

Chapter Two

Enhancing Learning in the Content Areas Through Discussion

When I try to convince teachers to add more discussion to their curriculum, they often tell me something along the lines of "Go back to your ivory tower! I do not have room to add one more thing!" or "If it's not on the end-of-grade tests, I don't have time for it" or "Sure, if you can find space for it in my day, because I can't." Once teachers have vented their justifiable frustrations, I talk to them, as I did to you in Chapter 1, about the importance of discussion as a means of engaging students in the higher-level thinking that constructs rich meaning and propels learning forward. Then I hit them hard with the real beauty of discussion, which is the focus of this chapter: Discussion neither takes away from nor adds to the curriculum. Rather, it supports it.

In this chapter, I emphasize discussion in reading, writing, science and health, social studies, literature studies, mathematics, and the arts as a means of learning both processes and content. First, I explore discussion as a tool that supports the curriculum without adding to it. Next, I look at how discussion can be used for various purposes within the curriculum, such as engaging students in learning, preparing them for reading and writing, and following up reading and writing. Then I give an overview of how to schedule discussion by weaving it into the curriculum. I conclude with a look at ways in which discussion may be used to promote learning in individual content areas.

Why Use Discussion Across the Curriculum?

Like reading and writing, discussion is not an end in itself and should not be taught in isolation. One discusses something for some purpose. Within the content areas, discussion has three main purposes:

1. **To lead students toward a particular curricular goal**
2. **To promote new insights**
3. **To guide students in discipline-specific ways of thinking**

Discussion Leads Students to a Curricular Goal

All content areas have important concepts that are critical for students to learn. These concepts are often at the heart of curricular goals, and discussion can focus on leading students toward meeting any goal, whether it's understanding metabolism, learning the relationship between weight and density, or coming to the conclusion that disagreement over the nature of states' rights, not slavery, was the fundamental cause of the American Civil War.

Leading students toward a particular goal calls for a different kind of discussion than allowing students to explore a topic freely. The questions you ask during the discussion are critical. Developing an effective set of questions takes time. Discussing those questions takes time, too.

Three basic rules of thumb in developing goal-oriented questions:

1. **Don't assume the students know where you are going.**
2. **Don't ask unrelated questions.** (You can always ask other questions at another time.) Unrelated questions confuse students and divert them from the goal.
3. **Don't try to get there too fast.** Ask questions that lead up to the "big" question, that help students go through the steps of the thinking required for success with the big question.

Let's look at two sets of questions designed to help students in a seventh-grade literature class reach the curricular goal of understanding that literature relates to their lives. The first set, the Ineffective Questions, does not get the job done, and my analysis describes which rules the questions violate. The second set, the Effective Questions, is a much more carefully developed group of questions. It took time to construct and order these questions, and it will take time for the students to discuss them.

Analysis of Ineffective and Effective Questions

Curricular Goal: Students will understand that literature relates to their lives by reading and discussing Gary Paulsen's *Hatchet* (1987).

Ineffective Questions

1. Have you ever faced a challenge?

2. Did you overcome the challenge?

Analysis

1. Students may not have a clear concept of *challenge* (violation of rules 1 and 3).

2. This is extraneous to the goal (violation of rule 2).

Effective Questions

1. What are some of the challenges Paul faced?

2. If students don't mention emotional challenges, such as loneliness or despair, ask: "What are some of the emotional challenges that Paul faced?"

3. Most of us have not been in plane crashes or lost in the wilderness for months, but all of us have faced challenges. What are some challenges you have faced?

Analysis

1. This helps students develop a concept of *challenge* (follows rule 1).

2. You are prepared if students mention only danger and other physical challenges (follows rule 1).

3. This develops the concept of *challenge* and asks students questions that lead them to connect literature to their lives (follows rule 3).

Why not just lecture if you want students to learn certain concepts or specific information? To be sure, lecture is often appropriate and can be a time-efficient means of conveying information. However, if students are just told information, they may not understand it or, even if they do, may not be able to retrieve it later. Discussion fosters engagement, construction of meaning, and higher-level thinking, which can result in a clearer understanding of concepts for all students. It also allows students to spend additional time on a topic, which can help them remember important ideas.

> "A teacher who tells students all about a subject offers only boredom. In addition, the students have been robbed of an opportunity to use their minds. All they have to do is soak up information and memorize it."
>
> – Leslie Trowbridge, Rodger Bybee, and Janet Powell

Discussion Promotes New Insights

One of the most important goals of any curriculum is to promote conceptual change: We want students to gain new insights, to expand upon those insights, to change as a result of exploring the content area. That's what education is all about!

Conceptual change comes about when students encounter internal or external conflict with their own thinking. Almasi (1995) calls this "sociocognitive conflict" and has identified three varieties of it:

◆ **Conflict within self.** This kind of conflict is confusion, when we don't know what we think. The confusion may be about something we have read or heard or our interpretation of it. We are aware that we don't understand something and seek clarification. I have conflict within myself every time I read the Internal Revenue Service's tax-preparation guidelines or my computer manual!

◆ **Conflict with others.** None of us is a stranger to this kind of conflict. For example, after reading the same novel, we find that someone else has an entirely different view of how the main character should have acted. After listening to the news, some of us may support the President and others may not, and most of us are passionate in our position. Conflict with others is a result of the vocal expression of ideas.

◆ **Conflict with text.** Conflict with text is a result of the written expression of ideas. Have you ever read something that completely contradicted your ideas? Of course you have. Whereas conflict with self is confusion, conflict with text is disagreement. You know what you think, but the ideas in the text voice a different opinion. Text often has more authority than the spoken word: "It's in a book (or on the Internet), so it must be true." It wasn't until I was a freshman in college that I understood that just because something is in print doesn't mean it's accurate. As teachers, we want to encourage students to see these kinds of challenges as opportunities to reflect and rethink ideas. Discussion can be an important tool in encouraging this process. Left alone with contradictions and challenges, a student may simply ignore them, and as a result, concepts remain unaltered. But when students are forced to respond to others' ideas through discussion, to defend their own thinking, to figure out why they think the way they do, the possibility for conceptual change, for new insights, is greatly increased.

> "Critical reflection . . . . requires not only that students thoughtfully reflect upon their own interpretations of text, but that they alter those interpretations when presented with conflicting evidence from the text or from their interpretative community."
>
> – Janice Almasi

Change does not necessarily mean the reversal of one's point of view. Sometimes a concept is altered greatly, sometimes it is refined, and sometimes it is even strengthened through an understanding of alternative points of view. But without discussion, the possibilities for conceptual change are diminished.

Discussion Guides Students in Discipline-Specific Ways of Thinking

Jerome Harste (1993) describes a content area as a lens through which one views an issue or a problem. A meteorologist, for example, views acid rain through the lens of science, which is a different lens than that of an economist, a mathematician, or a health educator. Each expert focuses on different data (the scientist may focus on the chemical aspects of acid rain, the economist on its financial impact, the mathematician on its likelihood in the future predictive models, and the health educator on its effects on humans). The processes of thinking also vary across content areas. Different disciplines have different ways of knowing, of gathering information, of privileging certain sources of data over others, and of drawing conclusions.

Discussion that is guided by carefully constructed and sequenced questions helps students develop discipline-specific ways of thinking. The purpose of such choreographed discussion is to lead the students toward a particular concept or conclusion and to show them how to think within this discipline. For example, the Effective Questions on page 23 lead students to define *challenge* by considering what happened to Paul in *Hatchet*, broadening their definitions as needed, and only then relating the novel to their own lives.

Here is one way to sequence questions to help students think in their discipline:

Step 1. Start with your goal, what you want the students to learn. Frame that goal as a question. Usually the goal question will require students to apply their knowledge and not just provide information they already know.

Goal: The students will be able to determine if an animal is a mammal.

Goal question: Is a rat a mammal?

Present the goal question to the students, but don't allow them to attempt to answer it immediately.

Step 2. Determine what the students need to consider to answer the goal question, and write one or more questions about that. These are foundation questions. The goal question may be very specific, but to answer it students have to consider the foundational concepts of the discipline. In this example, in order to answer the goal question, students need to think about what categorizes an animal as a mammal.

Foundation question: What are the characteristics of mammals?

Step 3. Tell students that the answer to the foundation question will help them answer the goal question. Ask them to apply their answer(s) to the foundation question to the goal question.

Answers to the foundation question may include:

Mammals have hair.

Mammals give birth to live young.

Mammals nurse their young.

Ask the students to apply each answer to rats. Do rats have hair? Give birth to live young? Nurse their young? Given the answers to these questions, return to the goal question: Is a rat a mammal? See the next page for another example.

How Can Discussion Be Used for Preparation and Follow-Up?

Discussion can take place at many different points in your teaching. You might have students engage in discussion just after you've introduced a topic. You might form discussion groups midway through a unit or as a culminating activity. The timing of discussion depends on the purpose. In this section, I look at using discussion for the following specific purposes: engaging students, preparing them for reading and for writing, and following up reading or writing.

EXAMPLE OF SEQUENCING QUESTIONS
IN A MATHEMATICS CLASS

Step 1

Goal: Students will be able to apply ratios to a real problem.

Goal question: We want to make this recipe for Supreme Chocolate Dessert. But we only have a nine-inch springform pan and the recipe calls for an eight-inch pan. How much of each ingredient should we use to fill the nine-inch pan to the proper level?

1 lb. sweet baking chocolate	2/3 c. butter, softened
1 T. flour (yes, just 1 tablespoon)	4 eggs, separated
1 T. sugar (ditto)	whipped cream

1. Line an eight-inch springform pan, sides and bottom, with waxed paper. (A little butter on the sides of the pan will help the paper stick.)
2. Melt the chocolate with 1 teaspoon water.
3. Remove from heat and stir in sugar, flour, and soft butter.
4. Beat egg yolks vigorously and stir into the chocolate mixture gradually and smoothly.
5. Beat mixture until it holds a peak and fold gently into the chocolate.
6. Spoon into pan and bake at 400°F for 20 minutes. It will be somewhat undercooked.

Step 2

Foundation question: What is the ratio of the volume of the two pans? Assume they are both two inches in height. (Students need to answer this question before they can answer the goal question.)

Step 3

Tell students, "Our goal question is: How much of each ingredient should we use? If you answer the foundation question—What is the ratio of the volume of the two pans?—you will have the information you need to find the answers to the goal question.

"The ratio between the two volumes is 127:100. Let's use that information to determine how much of each ingredient we should use."

Note: This is a real recipe for serious chocoholics. Enjoy!

Engaging Students

Discussion can help to engage students in three ways:

- Knowing they will have the opportunity (or challenge) of sharing information and solving a problem with others is motivating for some students. The chance to "strut their stuff" to an audience of peers may lead to more thoughtful work than, say, writing a report with the teacher as sole audience (Almasi & Gambrell, 1994).

- The very act of discussing can promote engagement (Almasi & Gambrell, 1994). The discussion provides a forum in which ideas can be presented, new information gained, and conclusions drawn. Hearing the ideas of others and having to defend one's own ideas can increase student interest in understanding a topic fully. Ideally, discussion promotes revision, which involves further engagement with the concepts under scrutiny.

- Discussion allows students to experience the thrill of discovery (Brumbaugh & Rock, 2001). Rather than being passive recipients of information conveyed by the teacher, students involved in discussion must do the cognitive work themselves and, in the process, learn that they can think, which enhances engagement.

Preparing Students For Reading

Typically, discussion is used as a follow-up activity after students have read an assignment. I explore that later, but in this section I focus on using discussion as a way to prepare students for successful reading. Prereading discussion can serve to determine what students know about the topic of the reading, let you introduce vocabulary, and prepare students to grapple with new or controversial ideas.

DETERMINE STUDENTS' BACKGROUND KNOWLEDGE

The quality and quantity of background knowledge that students bring to a text has a huge impact on their understanding of that text. For example, being aware of the social and historical contexts for Charles Dickens's novels will greatly enhance students' understanding of his works and their appreciation of them as social commentaries. Prereading discussion allows you to determine the

---

Questions for Stimulating Discussion About Prior Knowledge

- What do we already know about ___?
- Why do you think it is important that we know ___ before we read about ___?
- We have just learned about ___? What do you think that has to do with ___?
- Tell me three things you already know about this topic. Which of these three is the most important? Why?

background information that students hold and to fill in gaps in that knowledge as necessary. It is also likely to enhance their understanding and engage them right from the start. So, rather than having students read the first two chapters of *A Tale of Two Cities* and then talking about the French Revolution, you may lead a discussion on the French Revolution before the students read. Students may talk about what they know about the French Revolution, which side they might have been on, whether they would have had the courage to rise up, and so on. As you listen, you can assess the students' readiness to delve into Dickens's complex book. In sum, prereading discussion can call to mind what students already know about the topic, identify what they don't know, clarify what they are confused about, and fill in essential gaps in their knowledge.

INTRODUCE VOCABULARY

One of the joys and challenges of teaching is introducing new concepts and the words we use to describe those concepts. Each week, students encounter many new words in all subject areas, such as *meiosis*, *oxymoron*, and *quadratic equation*, and understanding their meanings is essential to understanding the concepts they represent. Writing an unfamiliar word on the board and exploring its meaning prepares students for successful reading and signals that the concept it represents is important. Reading a word explored in discussion reinforces understanding of that word during reading.

> ### Questions for Discussing Important Vocabulary
>
> Show the word in context. For example: "Carla was very <u>assertive</u> during the discussion. She really wanted to get her own way."
> - What do you think this word means? What makes you think that?
> - How is this word different in meaning from ___?
> - Can we substitute ___ for this word? Why? Why not?

BUILD AWARENESS OF CONTROVERSY OR ALTERNATE POINTS OF VIEW

When assigning a text that presents a controversial opinion, be sure to warn students of that fact. Doing so can promote critical reading of the text rather than passive acceptance or rejection of the author's opinion. Remember how embarrassed you were when you were taken in by something you read uncritically? Maybe it was an ad that promised you could lose ten pounds a week yet eat as much as you like. Or maybe it was a profile of a political candidate that you found out later was written by someone from the opposing party. Much of what students read is designed to be processed uncritically. For example, an account of who signed the Declaration of Independence or a description of England during Chaucer's time is fairly straightforward information and does not call on the students' critical reading skills. Since students may have developed a habit of reading uncritically, it is only fair to alert them to switch on their critical reading skills when you assign something that calls for those skills.

Preparing Students for Writing

What better preparation for writing is there than for students to think about what they want to say, figure out how they will support that, consider the reactions of others to their ideas, and come up with counterarguments? Discussion allows all that. Further, discussion can help writers sharpen their logic, refine their ideas, and even change their direction based on the views of others.

For a better idea of what I mean, read the following discussion among sixth-grade students who have been asked to write a persuasive essay about their choice of school mascot. Figure 2-1 shows each student's planning before the discussion begins.

JERRY: I want the cobra! Cool!

MELISSA: Cool? Yuck. What's cool about a snake?

JERRY: You know. Just think of the T-shirts we could have, with a big old snake with blood dripping from its fangs. Cool.

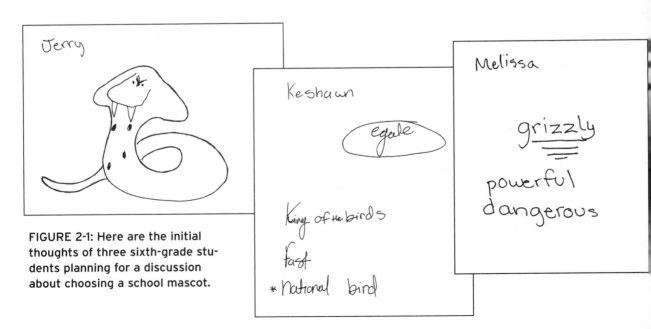

FIGURE 2-1: Here are the initial thoughts of three sixth-grade students planning for a discussion about choosing a school mascot.

KESHAWN: I want the eagle. It's the king of birds, the fiercest.

MELISSA: I think the mascot should be the grizzly because it's such a strong, powerful animal. We want our school to seem powerful.

KESHAWN: Yeah, powerful is good. But the eagle is powerful and it's fast. The grizzly's slow.

MELISSA: Oh no it's not! Last week on the Discovery Channel I watched a grizzly go after a baby moose. That bear moved! And we could have a big roar as part of our cheer.

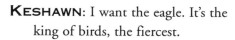

ACTIVITY

Buzz Groups

Divide the class into groups of three to five, with each group composed of students of varied reading abilities, background knowledge, and confidence levels. Have the groups discuss their initial responses to one of the questions that appear in the box on page 30. After five minutes, have the groups report their findings and any questions they want answered (modified from Dynneson & Gross, 1995).

KESHAWN: I think eagles make a really scary sound. Don't they call it their war cry?

MELISSA: Jerry, somehow "hisssss" isn't so great as a cheer!

JERRY: But think of the T-shirts!

KESHAWN: The eagle is our national bird.

MELISSA: Isn't it supposed to stand for bravery? That's a good thing. But since the eagle is already kind of our mascot, because we are Americans, let's do something different and go with the grizzly.

Figure 2-2 shows how the students' thinking changed as a result of the discussion. Poor Jerry realizes that he has only one argument, and no one is buying it. He starts over with a new animal and with a few ideas gleaned from the discussion. Melissa has learned that she needs to correct the misconception that grizzlies are slow. She adds the roar as a cheer, which is something she thought of during the discussion. And Keshawn's choice of the eagle has led Melissa to plan to write about how the grizzly provides a new symbol for the school, whereas the eagle repeats an existing American symbol. Melissa actually gave Keshawn several new ideas, including using an animal sound as a cheer and recognizing the mascot as a symbol of power. Keshawn takes Melissa's comment about the eagle as a symbol of bravery, layers on thoughts about his uncle's service in the army, and decides to stress a patriotic theme.

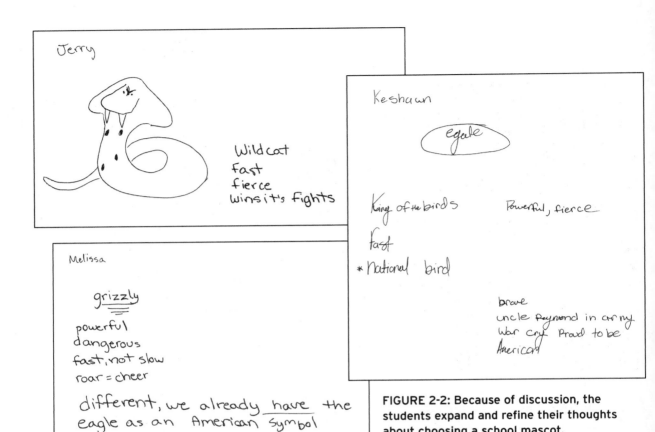

FIGURE 2-2: Because of discussion, the students expand and refine their thoughts about choosing a school mascot.

Discussion Webs

According to Donna Alvermann (1991), a discussion web teaches students "to look at both sides of an issue before drawing conclusions" (p. 92). Here's how you might use a discussion web in your classroom:

1. Have individual students think about a couple of possible responses to a central content-area question. For example, for social studies, ask, "Should the U.S. adopt a national health

care system?" For science, ask, "Should the government support stem-cell research?"

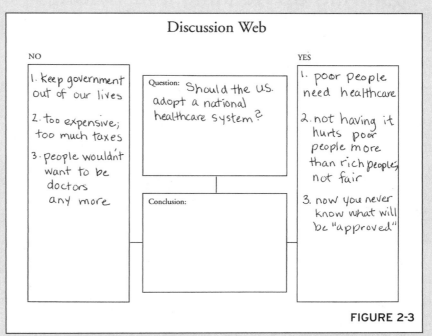

FIGURE 2-3

Discussion Web

NO

1. Keep government out of our lives
2. too expensive; too much taxes
3. people wouldn't want to be doctors any more

Question: Should the U.S. adopt a national healthcare system?

Conclusion:

YES

1. poor people need healthcare
2. not having it hurts poor people more than rich people; not fair
3. now you never know what will be "approved"

2. In pairs, have students share their responses to the question and identify two conflicting points of view even if both partners have the same point of view.

3. Ask partners to take turns providing an equal number of reasons to support each point of view and write them down in the appropriate sections of the web. (See Figure 2-3.) This forces students to look at both sides of the issue.

4. Once the web is completed, ask partners to join another pair of students to compare their reasons and work toward consensus to come to a group conclusion. Each member of the group does not need to agree with the conclusion but must be able to provide reasons that support the conclusion.

5. Once the conclusion is reached, have the group quickly identify the one reason that best supports their conclusion. In a whole-class discussion, a spokesperson for each group presents its conclusion and supporting reason.

Creating this kind of discussion web provides students with a conclusion and a rationale that supports that conclusion. Furthermore, by knowing the rationale that supports a different point of view, students understand what they need to refute in a discussion or in an essay (Alvermann, 1991). (See Appendix 1 for a reproducible template of a discussion web.)

Following Up Reading and Writing

Postreading and postwriting discussion serves many important functions. Students review ideas (Leal, 1993), distinguishing between important and less important ones (Almasi, 1995). From there, they can synthesize what they have learned into major concepts, rather than being left with a set of interesting facts that don't add up to much (Gilles, 1993; Jacque, 1993). They can clarify and revise their ideas (Almasi, 1995; Short, 1993). They can reach deeper meanings (Almasi, 1995; Peterson & Eeds, 1990) and higher levels of thinking (Anzul, 1993; Cox & Many, 1992).

LISTENING IN

For two weeks, keep track of discussion that takes place in your classroom. Are there true discussions, as defined in Chapter 1? How does discussion arise? What provokes discussion? What are the purposes of discussion? The answers to these questions will allow you to think about whether you are providing enough opportunities for discussion and if those discussions serve curricular goals.

To gather information, you might want to use a form like the one shown in Figure 2-4. A blank, reproducible version of this form is in Appendix 2. Of course, you can also develop your own form.

Listening In on Discussion Form

Date *Nov. 18*   Participants *whole class*

Focus of Discussion
whether the school should buy new bike racks

How did the discussion start?
☐ I gave an assignment to discuss.
    My purpose:

☐ I asked a question.
    Did I intend this to provoke a discussion or just to get an answer?

☐ _____ asked a question.

☒ **Other:** *Jamaal was angry that his bike was stolen because not enough racks*

What was the purpose of the discussion?
The class wanted to write a letter to the principal about this.

FIGURE 2-4

What Time Factors Must Be Considered for Discussion to Work?

According to Carol Fuhler (1994), "when you first ask students what they think, they often don't know" (p. 403). You are likely to get a startled look, a shrug, and a grunt. And to make matters more frustrating, often students think they are now off the hook! If you persist in trying to wheedle answers out of them, they may view you as being mean and unfair. Alas, the ability to discuss does not spring forth spontaneously from most students. It takes time: sufficient time across the school year to develop effective strategies; time each week to practice those strategies; and time for discussion groups, where students can apply those strategies.

Time to Develop Effective Strategies

Discussion strategies develop; they do not just show up one day fully formed. Even adults often are not very good at discussion, and students, to be sure, have to learn strategies that promote effective discussion, such as

◆ listening to others with an open mind;
◆ viewing others as sources of information and not just as an audience for one's own views;
◆ being willing to rethink and revise after listening to others;
◆ finding a focus for discussion;
◆ refocusing as needed;
◆ learning how to stay on task;
◆ trusting one's self as a thinker and trusting others to respect those thoughts even if they disagree;
◆ developing the courage to speak up with a new idea, a challenge, an offer of support
(see Chapter 3 for more information on many of the above strategies);
◆ accepting the transfer of the responsibility for good discussion from the teacher to the students;
◆ learning how to facilitate and participate in discussions without the teacher's guiding hand
(see Chapter 4 for more information on the last two strategies).

All of these strategies develop over time as students gain discussion experience. Peterson and Eeds (1990) urge us to accept approximations in the process: "Competence is achieved over time, and we concern ourselves in the direction of the responses children make . . . . every bit as much as with the specific content of those responses" (p. 23).

"Just Go Discuss"

Introducing discussion to students by telling them to "just go discuss" is a guarantee of failure because, as we have seen, most students don't know how to discuss. Poor direction like that will lead not to discussion, but to conversation, reporting, and lecturing, and over time students may feel that they are not capable of true discussion. A more effective approach is to gradually hand over control to students, with lots of modeling of appropriate and inappropriate discussion strategies. You might follow this progression:

1. **Several teacher-led whole-group discussions on strategies.** After each discussion, have a discussion about the discussion to determine what worked and what didn't work. (See example on page 37.)

2. **A few small-group discussions based on a question chosen by you.** Pay a short visit to each group. Reassemble the class after small-group discussions to discuss their level of success.

3. **Two or three small-group discussions based on a topic chosen by group members.** Reassemble the class after small-group discussions to identify problems and propose solutions.

Harvey Daniels (2002), well known for his work on literature discussion, suggests the use of roles to scaffold the development of discussion strategies. Rotating roles, such as Literary Luminary and Questioner, help students take on the responsibilities of running a discussion and focusing on different perspectives. The Word Wizard's role is to find words in the selection that have special meaning or stand out for some reason, find their definitions, and help the group locate and discuss the words. In this role, the student becomes aware of the importance of vocabulary in the construction of meaning. Daniels sees these roles as temporary, as a way to support students as they develop the skills and habits of effective discussion. Once these strategies and habits are internalized, assigning roles is no longer necessary.

A TEACHER-LED WHOLE-GROUP DISCUSSION ABOUT A DISCUSSION

In this discussion, Jeni Day and her fifth graders talk about Chris Van Allsburg's *The Wretched Stone* (1991), a fantasy about a group of sailors who bring a large, glowing stone aboard their ship after discovering it on a deserted island. The stone has a powerful effect on the sailors: it mesmerizes them, turns them into monkeys, and serves as an intriguing metaphor to focus on in classroom discussion. As you read the example, think about what is working well and what isn't working so well. Then see my thoughts at the end.

Before reading the book to the class, Jeni asked students to think about what the author was trying to tell them by writing this book. We pick up the discussion after she has finished the book and the students have written their answers to the question.

JENI: Our prompt was: "What do you think the author was trying to tell you by writing this book?" Does anyone have some thoughts on this? Listen to each other and see if that helps your own answer.

CASSY: Sometimes shipping . . .

JENI: I don't think everyone can hear you. Speak louder.

CASSY: Sometimes shipping is dangerous.

JENI: Did you all hear that?

CLASS: No.

CASSY: *[speaks louder]* Sometimes shipping is dangerous.

JENI: Someone else?

ROY: Don't take something from the island that's strange.

KAYLA: If something bad happens . . .

JENI: Did you hear that, Larry? You're right next to Kayla and you're not paying attention.

KAYLA: If something bad happens, you just got to work through it.

JENI: Okay. Artie?

ARTIE: Appearances can be deceiving.

ABDUL: You can get sick if you do bad things.

JENI: The whole point of this is to listen to each other. Raise your hand if you think you are listening to each other.

ELLA: It's kind of like what Kayla said, that even though something bad happens, you work at it and it will turn out all right.

MEIKO: It's kind of like Cassy said—if there is a place and stuff that you are unfamiliar with, it might not be very safe to take something from it. The other thing was maybe if you are smart and know how to read, it will be better because in the book they said that the ones that knew how to read, like . . . *[stops talking]*

JENI: Did the author say anything else about reading?

[The class comments on how the readers in the book recovered quickly.]

JENI: Do you think the author was trying to tell you something about reading?

CASSY: I think he's saying that reading is good.

JENI: When do reading and things like that come into the story?

JASMINE: When the captain writes in his log.

ABDUL: When they had free time, it said they read a lot.

BETTY: They told stories.

JENI: That's good. Let me go ahead and tell you that this story is an analogy, which means that things in the story stand for something else. Can you think of anything that the rock, the wretched stone, stands for?

ARTIE: It might be a bad luck sign.

JENI: Did you all hear that?

CLASS: No.

ARTIE: I said, it might be a bad luck sign.

[The class has a discussion about what it means to be smart. Jeni tries to lead them to focus on what happened when the sailors watched the stone. The class can repeat what happened, but they are not coming up with the higher-level thinking needed to arrive at an analogy. Finally . . .]

CASSY: I think the author was saying, be constructive or be punished. I mean, don't just sit around and watch TV or sit around and watch the rock and not just work at all. If you do, you could get punished.

If you led this discussion, what would you focus on to help the students develop better strategies? One answer is *listening*. The fact that they seldom followed up on one another's comments tells me that they weren't listening closely to one another. Jeni often had to remind the students to do that, despite the advice on successful listening that she gave them before reading. (This is not surprising. Most students find it difficult to develop good listening habits, even with help from the teacher.) When students did follow up on one another's comments, true discussion ensued.

Another aspect of this discussion worth pointing out is the level of thinking it required. It was hard for the class to understand Van Allsburg's analogy. Perhaps a mini-lesson on analogies before listening to the story would have moved the class more quickly to the higher-level thinking Jeni sought.

> "If students come upon a troublesome issue in their literature study or other study groups, we can't expect a single group conversation to settle the question in their minds. Readers may continue to mull over the problem at home and at school, trying out options and looking back or asking others for various solutions."
>
> – Carol Gilles

Time Each Week to Practice Strategies

Your students won't develop and maintain good discussion strategies through "discussion units" a couple of times a year. Discussion should be a routine, predictable part of the weekly, if not the daily, curriculum so that every student in the class gets plenty of practice. In addition, when you include discussion in the weekly schedule, you send a strong message to students that you respect discussion and think it is worth the time. Discussion becomes a genuine, valued part of the curriculum. See Figures 2-5 and 2-6 for sample schedules.

FOURTH-GRADE SOCIAL STUDIES

MONDAY
1:00–1:30: Prepare for discussion about slavery. Do Background Knowledge Quiz* and then discuss. Have class set one or two purposes for studying slavery.

TUESDAY
During reading time and also 1:00–1:30: Choose from our social studies text (pp. 45–50), or <u>Follow the Drinking Gourd</u>, <u>Papa John</u>, or pp. 12–13 in <u>NC History</u> magazine (field slaves vs. house slaves).

WEDNESDAY
Sometime: Respond in journal: Why did "good" people have slaves?

THURSDAY
1:00–1:30: Small-group discussion based on what was read, to answer: (1) What was it like to be a house slave? (2) What was it like to be a field slave? (3) Would you have owned slaves? Why or why not? (4) If you had been a slave, would you have run away? Why or why not? 1:30–2:00: whole-class discussion of the four questions.

FRIDAY
Sometime: Have students write in journal any new thoughts about slavery.

* See page 60 for information on Background Knowledge Quiz.

FIGURE 2-5: Finding time for discussion in social studies: a sample schedule.

SEVENTH-GRADE SCIENCE

FRIDAY

Find out what they know about rocks by doing a K–W–L assessment.* Homework: Chapter 7.

MONDAY

20 min.: Divide class into 6 groups. 2 groups will discuss igneous rocks, 2 groups will discuss sedimentary, and 2 will discuss metamorphic. Each group will fill in this chart for its rock type:

Type of rock	How it's formed	Types/groups	Uses

10 min.: Combine groups on each type of rock and come to agreement on the chart.

10 min.: Write in journal: Why is my rock type important?

TUESDAY

50 min.: Whole group—fill in class chart; hold a discussion about why each type of rock is important.

WEDNESDAY

Lab: Classify rocks by type. Each group has to come to agreement as they rotate through the stations.

THURSDAY

15 min.: Journal: What is the most important type of rock?

15 min.: Whole-class discussion of journal response.

20 min.: Start on erosion. Do List-Group-Label.†

* The rest of the plan was developed after the K-W-L assessment. See page 65 (Figure 3-5) for information on K-W-L.

† See page 61 (Figure 3-2) for information on List-Group-Label.

FIGURE 2-6: Finding time for discussion in science: a sample schedule.

Time for Applying Strategies in Discussion Groups

Here are guidelines for getting discussion groups up and running in your classroom:

1. Schedule discussion groups. Block out the time in your plan book. Finding the time for true discussion is complicated. Different groups of students will need different amounts of time, and certain topics will require more time than others. So be flexible. For example, rather than allotting 9:00–9:40 for discussion and expecting it to take up that amount of time and no more, you might give two or three different assignments across two 40-minute periods: a discussion and two other activities, such as free-reading or free-writing or working on a research report. If the discussion takes both 40-minute periods for some groups, then that's what it takes. If it takes only 20 minutes for one group, then those students can turn to one of the other important activities. Trying to cram all discussions into one time frame will rarely result in productive discussions for all. If Jeni had allotted only 10 minutes for the discussion of *The Wretched Stone*, the students never would have discovered the central analogy of the story.

2. Plan time for preparation, reflection, and follow-up. Preparation may take place the day before, and should be individually paced. Students can prepare independently in various ways, such as writing in a journal or reading a text. Finding large chunks of time necessary for some aspects of the follow-up may be more difficult. Be creative in your scheduling. For example, you may do a "double dose" of science on Wednesday so that on Thursday you can skip science and give students the amount of time they need for a true discussion and follow-up. Or if you are restricted to a 55-minute class schedule, spread the lesson across three days: preparation on Monday, discussion on Tuesday, and follow-up on Wednesday.

3. Give ample time for each discussion. Use your best judgment, and then add time! Follow the advice under guideline 1, but be flexible, if possible. Students can always move to an ongoing assignment, if their group finishes earlier than you planned.

Keep in mind, true discussion wanders, goes down false paths, explores tentative ideas, and constructs meaning from the contributions of many. Without the time for participants to challenge ideas, ask questions, focus and refocus, gather the courage to speak, and revise their thoughts, discussion may be superficial and arid. If we allow only a small amount of time for a discussion, we send a message that the topic is not important or that there is one right answer to be found, and found quickly. Genuine questions require genuine discussion. Important topics take time to identify and explore.

4. Don't ask for final thoughts until the students have had time to reflect and revise their thinking. Give students a day to do that rethinking. One purpose of discussion is to learn what others think, to share one's own ideas, and to rethink those ideas. Rethinking and revision take reflection.

"Hurry Up!"

The most effective discussions are not placed under time constraints. After all, how can we identify the exact amount of time needed for participants to share ideas, challenge each other, and revise their thoughts? Benny's group may need 10 minutes and Selina's group 30. And, of course, our reality is that the bell is going to ring in 15 minutes or the music teacher is arriving in five. Here are a couple of ways to avoid hovering around a discussion, urging the students to "Hurry up!"

◆ Never let a group start a discussion with only a short amount of time left. It is better to have the discussion the next day than to rush through it.

◆ Come prepared with worthwhile assignments for those who finish early, such as independent reading or writing. Resist saying, "Get started on your homework," which can lead students to either linger in their groups to avoid homework or rush the discussion in order to finish their homework before leaving school.

And reflection takes time. Jerome Harste, Katherine Short, and Carolyn Burke (1988) call this "time to absorb and savor." In that time, students gain ownership of ideas and consolidate their thinking.

Discussion in Individual Content Areas

Jerome Harste (1993) reminds us that each content area has its own way of exploring issues and solving problems. The nature of thinking in science is different from the nature of thinking in art. A discussion about the Constitutional Convention will proceed in a much different manner than a discussion of sexist themes in *Cinderella* or effective ways to solve a word problem. One of our most important roles as teachers is to help students develop the ways of thinking in the various content areas. Discussion is a natural forum for practicing them.

In this section, I move from general curriculum issues to showing how discussion can enhance learning in science and health, social studies, literature, mathematics, and the arts. Although you may be more interested in some content areas than others, at least skim each section because a suggestion made for one content area is likely to be germane to others. Leslie Trowbridge, Rodger

Bybee, and Janet Powell (2000) point out that it is important for information exchanged during science discussions to be accurate, and this, of course, is true for all content areas. Students should not merely exchange "facts" and call it discussion, but the information they use to hypothesize, predict, argue, persuade, and synthesize during a discussion is only valuable if it's true. Although incorrect information can spur discussion, it is detrimental if it is accepted as fact. The conclusions that students draw, and even the logic of the discussion, will most likely be false.

So how can you ensure accuracy in discussion? If it's a whole-class discussion with you presiding, the task is fairly simple. With your store of expert knowledge, you can identify incorrect information and provide clarification. This can be done without damaging a student's self-esteem if you also acknowledge what that student does correctly.

Comments such as these can be helpful in focusing students on the importance of "truth in discussion":

◆ **Right logic, wrong information:** "Lamont is certainly on the right track when he says that smoking can cause lung cancer. But he's gone a little too far when he says smoking is the only cause of lung cancer, even when you take secondhand smoke into consideration. Lung cancer can also be caused by . . ."

◆ **Right logic, incomplete information:** "I like the way you are thinking, Rhonda. Here is some information that can make your argument even stronger. Did you know that . . . ."

◆ **Valid attempt, wrong information and, therefore, invalid conclusion:** Try the good news/bad news approach, first commenting on what the student did well and then pointing out what was wrong or needs to be improved. "Mai Ling, I can see why you think that we should kill all the snakes we find in our gardens. But you are basing that conclusion on a faulty piece of information. It is not true that all snakes are poisonous. In fact, most snakes in our area are not poisonous. And since believing that all snakes are poisonous is your main reason for thinking we should kill them, we cannot conclude that killing all snakes is the right thing to do."

In small-group discussion, however, you are usually not there to monitor the accuracy of the information being exchanged. Here are two tactics that may help participants do that for themselves.

Students need to be able to spot incorrect information and challenge it in socially acceptable ways. Comments like "That is *so* wrong!" and "Where did you get such a stupid idea?!" certainly won't encourage a healthy interchange of ideas. But here are a few comments that might: "You know, I'm pretty sure that's not right." "I don't think I agree. Do you remember where you got that information or why you think that?" "Are you sure that's right? I thought ___. How can we figure out which one of us has the right information?" Teach students to disagree agreeably.

A Confidence Rating Form is useful when you suspect that students may be working with incomplete or incorrect information. (See Figure 2-7 and Appendix 3.) Ask students to fill one out cooperatively at the end of their discussion. At the bottom of the form, students write a conclusion to their discussion. In the boxes above, they list all the points that led them to make that conclusion. For each entry students rate their confidence about its accuracy:

◆ 3 = "We are very sure this is true."
◆ 2 = "We think this is true."
◆ 1 = "We are unsure if this is true."

Filling out the Confidence Rating Form also helps students understand that the strength of their conclusion is only as strong as the facts and assumptions that led to it.

What does discussion look like in individual content areas?

Confidence Rating Form

Information Leading to Our Conclusion	Confidence Rating
income from Bob's job = $37,000 income from Mary Sue's job = 28,000	3
deduct cost of new car as business expense	1
deduct mortgage interest	2
tax rate = 27%	2
Conclusion: Bob + Mary Sue owe $9,450 in federal taxes	2

FIGURE 2-7: This form helps students think about their confidence in the information they use to draw conclusions.

In the sections that follow, I answer that question. I first describe the ways of thinking for each content area and then offer ideas for applying those ways of thinking in discussion.

Ways of Thinking in Science and Health

Do you recall the definition of the scientific method that you learned years ago? It probably went something like this: (1) identify a purpose, (2) form a hypothesis, (3) gather data, (4) analyze the data, and (5) come to a conclusion. But thinking in science is richer than this and not nearly as linear. Rather, it is made up of a dazzling array of processes (from Lemke, 1990, p. ix):

observing	analyzing	challenging	concluding
describing	discussing	arguing	generalizing
comparing	hypothesizing	justifying	reporting
deciding	theorizing	designing experiments	
classifying	questioning	following procedures	

What fun!

GETTING DISCUSSION STARTED IN SCIENCE AND HEALTH

So how can discussion promote these wonderful ways of thinking? Science and health are full of controversy, and we all know that nothing sparks a discussion like controversy. For example, asking students to take a stand on tapping the oil reserves in Alaska, or using nuclear energy to power residential areas, is guaranteed to provoke discussion and engage students in scientific ways of thinking. Controversial issues are especially effective opportunities for practicing the civility necessary for good discussion. But always be careful with a controversial issue that your own perspectives are not privileged. Controversy is fabulous for generating discussion, but you need to be vigilant that all sides get a fair hearing and that civility is maintained. And since the teacher's opinion can carry quite a bit of weight, it's best that your views remain unknown.

Here are some other ideas:

◆ **Draw on the interrelationships between science and technology and society** (Trowbridge et al., 2000). For example, ask, "Just because we are able to clone animals, should we? Through genetic engineering we can produce mildew-resistant tomatoes. What are the dangers of genetically engineering plants, if any?"

◆ **Explore the unsolved problems of science and health.** By doing so, you provide students with opportunities to hypothesize and use their scientific knowledge to design experiments that might lead to resolutions. Ask questions such as, "How can we make prescription drugs affordable?" and "What do we know about cell division that might lead to a cure for cancer?

◆ **Provide demonstrations.** Science is full of mysterious wonders that at first glance often don't make sense. Predicting what will happen and hypothesizing about why it happened will lead to interesting and productive discussions. See the sample demonstration on the next page.

> " 'Talking science' means writing, lecturing, and teaching in and through the language of science."
>
> – Jay Lemke

For How Long Can You Boil Water in a Paper Cup?

This activity will generate interest, wonder, and much discussion among middle school students.

I. CONCEPTS

◆ A flame is a source of radiant heat.

◆ Water, when heated, expands and gives off water vapor.

◆ Water can absorb a considerable amount of heat.

◆ Before a substance will burn, its kindling temperature must be reached.

◆ The kindling temperature is the temperature at which a substance will first start to burn.

II. MATERIALS

Unwaxed paper cup

Bunsen burner, propane torch, or alcohol burner ring stand

Ring clamp

Wire screen

III. PRELABORATORY DISCUSSION

To engage students, focus them on the relevant chemical processes, and encourage them to participate in the scientific process, ask these questions:

1. What do you think will happen to a paper cup when you try to boil water in it?
2. Do you think the water will boil before the cup burns, or vice versa?
3. How do you think you could get a paper cup containing water to burn?
4. What could you do to find out?

IV. LABORATORY ACTIVITY

1. Show students the materials listed above.
2. Ask students, "How could you use this equipment to find out whether you can boil

water in a paper cup?"

3. If students cannot think of ways to boil the water using the materials, then show them a diagram and set up the equipment accordingly.

4. Have students place the paper cup, containing not more than five centimeters of water, on the wire screen and heat it from below with the burner.

5. Periodically touch the paper cup and report any change of temperature to the class.

6. Ask students the following questions:
   ◆ What happens when you try to heat the water in the cup?
   ◆ What do you think the ring clamp and screen do to the heat from the flame?
   ◆ What can you say about the heat energy entering and leaving the water as you try to heat it to the boiling point?
   ◆ Why does the water level in the cup change?
   ◆ What effect does the water in the cup have on the cup's temperature as it is being heated?

7. Keep heating the cup until all the water is evaporated. Have students record their observations and conclusions.

V. OPEN-ENDED QUESTIONS

Divide the class into five groups and assign one question to each group. After five minutes, ask each group to explain its answer.

1. If you heated paper, cloth, wood, and charcoal, in what order would they start to burn? Why?

2. If you were going to repeat the preceding experiment, what would you do to obtain better data?

3. How would the results be affected if you used a Styrofoam cup?

4. How could varying the amount of heat energy applied to the cup change the results?

5. How would the results vary if there were a different liquid in the cup, such as cola or syrup? Why?

Adapted from Trowbridge, L., Bybee, R., & Powell, J. (2000). *Teaching secondary science*. Upper Saddle River, NJ: Prentice-Hall.

Ways of Thinking in Social Studies

History, geography, economics, sociology, anthropology—there are millions of interesting facts to learn about these subjects. And students are intrinsically drawn to learning that Henry VIII had six wives or that the Masai drink blood. But as delightful as that information is, amassing a collection of unrelated facts is not what social studies are all about. Memorizing facts is not thinking, and the social studies are about big ideas and issues that require sophisticated thought: decision-making, inquiring, analyzing, problem-solving, and reflecting. These are the skills informed citizens use to analyze and solve dilemmas past, present, and future.

> "The key goal of discussion is to practice cooperative deliberation and group thinking toward problem resolution or best possible answers."
>
> – Thomas Dynneson and Richard Gross

GETTING DISCUSSION STARTED IN SOCIAL STUDIES

As with controversies in science, controversies in social studies help students develop the problem-solving skills critical for becoming citizens in a democratic society. Topics such as capital punishment, the war with Iraq, the suspension of civil liberties during wartime, and government invasion of privacy provide opportunities for students to use analytic and problem-solving skills in discussion. Encourage students to do the following:

◆ Challenge preconceived notions. For example, many believe that the cause of the American Civil War was slavery, but is that true? Many believe that the United States is a democracy, but is that true? Questions like these provide the opportunity for rich discussion, as students explore why they hold beliefs and what information contradicts their beliefs.

◆ Reconsider options of the past to inform the present and the future. The philosopher George Santayana said, "Those who cannot remember the past are condemned to repeat it." The study of history is the examination of options and consequences. What lessons from the Holocaust can we apply to ethnic cleansing in central Europe? What did we learn from the Treaty of Versailles about the humiliation of being on the losing side in a war? What might King George have done differently to prevent the American Revolution?

Ways of Thinking About Literature

Discussion about literature is unlike discussion in other content areas because there are two distinctly different purposes to discussion: discussing responses to literature and studying literature. Sometimes students discuss their personal responses to what they have read. In this case, the focus is

Semantic Webbing: Organizing Facts

The purpose of semantic webbing is to guide students toward organizing facts into concepts, to show how information fits together to form big ideas (Freedman & Reynolds, 1980).

1. **Come up with a question that does not have a clear answer and will spark several different points of view.** For example, ask "What should the U.S. have done when Germany prepared to annex Czechoslovakia in 1938?" Write the question in the middle of the chalkboard or a large sheet of paper.
2. **Elicit answers from the class.** Ask "Why?" as necessary to prompt students to explain their reasoning. Write all answers around the central question: *send troops, bomb Germany, negotiate.*
3. **Ask students to link the different responses conceptually.** Have them suggest relationships between the answers that get at some of the content area's big ideas, not just its facts: "Which of your proposed actions are short-term solutions and which are long-term solutions?" The most interesting discussion often occurs at this point.

Semantic webbing is a great way to move from bits of information to issues and concepts.

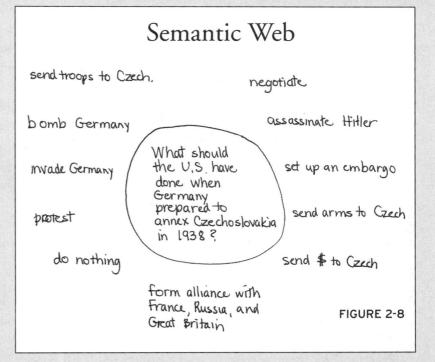

Semantic Web

send troops to Czech.

negotiate

bomb Germany

assassinate Hitler

invade Germany

What should the U.S. have done when Germany prepared to annex Czechoslovakia in 1938?

set up an embargo

protest

send arms to Czech

do nothing

send $ to Czech

form alliance with France, Russia, and Great Britain

FIGURE 2-8

on what Louise Rosenblatt (1978) calls the aesthetic stance to reading, the experience of making personal connections with the text. In this type of discussion, experiencing and reflecting are important ways of thinking. I remember how angry Mildred Taylor's *Roll of Thunder, Hear My Cry* (1976) made me feel because of the injustices suffered by blacks during the Depression, and how surprised I was when many undergraduate students of education didn't share that anger. Our varied responses fueled an illuminating discussion that reminded me that what the reader brings to the piece of literature is as important as what the literature brings to the reader.

Literature discussion groups can also center on a piece of literature as a crafted work, as a product of its time and of its author, and as a form of writing. Discussions for these purposes call upon students to use their interpretation and analysis skills. Students may talk about analogy in C. S. Lewis's *The Lion, the Witch, and the Wardrobe* (1950), the connections between Edgar Allan Poe's dark life and his dark writing, or character development in Harper Lee's *To Kill a Mockingbird* (1960).

GETTING LITERATURE DISCUSSION STARTED

The personal connections a reader makes to literature lead naturally to lively discussion because those connections are so personal and varied. For example, a student who has spent a lot of time camping will connect with Gary Paulsen's *Hatchet* (1987) much differently than a student who has purposefully avoided camping. I've always had a fond feeling for Shel Silverstein's "Sick" (1974) because the poem captures exactly the fruitless negotiations I had with my mother when I didn't want to go to school. What wonderful discussions my mother and I could've had about this poem when I was a child. Here are some ways to spark discussion about literature. (The first three are modified from Day, Spiegel, McLellan, & Brown, 2002.):

◆ **Encourage students to offer their own responses and embrace different ones.** Students are often surprised when others don't have the same reaction to a story or poem as they do. Discussion of the reasons for those different reactions helps students understand the personal nature of responses to literature. Readers who have never lost a beloved pet are less likely to sob at the end of *Where the Red Fern Grows* (Rawls, 1961), as I did. I have never dared to read *Old Yeller* (Gipson, 1956) or *Sounder* (Armstrong, 1969).

◆ **Ask students to identify important elements in a story or poem.** Ask: *Who was the most important character in this story? What makes you think so? What surprised you in this story? Why was that a surprise? What did you expect instead?* Questions like these will spark true discussion because opinions will vary so widely (Graham & Spiegel, 1996).

◆ **Urge students to notice the author's craft.** Discussion of how the author developed characters or built suspense or injected humor leads to insights about how literature is crafted. For example, students can explore the use of repetition in Dr. Seuss's *The 500 Hats of Bartholomew Cubbins* (1938) as a means of creating suspense. (Each hat is more elaborate than the next, lead-

ACTIVITY

Fishbowl

This activity has many purposes. It builds discussion and observation skills, builds content knowledge, and gets students thinking about their level and quality of participation in group discussions (from Baloche, Mauger, Willis, Filinuk, & Michalsky, 1993).

1. Seat the students in two concentric circles and pair each student in the inner circle with one in the outer circle.
2. Pose a thought-provoking discussion question to students in the inner circle. For example, after reading *The Midwife's Apprentice* (Cushman, 1995), sixth graders might discuss, "What part of life in the Middle Ages would you have disliked the most? Is there some aspect of that life you would have liked a lot?"
3. As the inner circle discusses the question, have each outer-circle student make notes on the discussion behavior of the inner-circle partner.
4. After the discussion, ask outer-circle students to give constructive feedback to their partners. For example, one student might note that her partner interrupted other speakers frequently. Another student might point out that his partner rarely expressed personal ideas and, instead, just agreed automatically with what others said.
5. Have partners exchange seats, and pose a new question.

ing readers to wonder, Where is this all leading?) This type of discussion also prompts students to try the techniques in their own writing.

◆ **Immerse students in the context and culture that inspired the literature.** Students may gain a richer understanding of Madeleine L'Engle's *A Wrinkle in Time* (1962) if they connect it to the cold war and the totalitarianism of the Soviet Union.

Ways of Thinking in Mathematics

Mathematics used to be about memorizing number facts, procedures, and formulas. Discussion wasn't a natural part of the mathematics curriculum because, by and large, students were taught one way to figure out problems. If there is one right way to solve a problem, then what is there to discuss? Times have changed, thank goodness. Current mathematics instruction focuses less on facts, procedures, and formulas and more on mathematical reasoning. Although there may be one right answer to a problem, there are likely to be many correct ways to get to that answer. The thinking of mathematics involves problem-solving, invention, reconceptualization, exploration, risk-taking, and persuasion. Discussion revolves around convincing others of the validity of a particular approach to solving a problem.

Let's try this out. Add these numbers and think about your process:

67   15   29   11   53

Time's up. Did you get 175, the correct answer? If so, we have nothing to discuss about that. But we have plenty to discuss about how you got that answer. Did you add the 1's column sequentially (7 + 5 + 9 + 1 + 3), put down the 1's numeral (5), and carry the 2 to the 10's column? That's probably what you were taught to do as a child. Until I discussed this process with someone, I always thought that's how I added. But I often don't. I usually look for sets that add to 10. So in the 1's column I added 7+3 and 9+1, making 20, and then added the 5 that hadn't been used yet. Discussion helped me become aware of what I actually was doing—and perhaps through this "discussion" you learned a quicker way to add.

GETTING DISCUSSION STARTED IN MATHEMATICS

For mathematics, there is one basic way to get students thinking and talking: Pose a problem that doesn't have one obvious solution or an obvious path to a solution. Here's an example:

> Suppose you have 64 meters of fence with which you are going to build a pen for your large dog, Bones. What are some different pens you can make if you use all the fencing? What is the pen with the least play space? What is the biggest pen you can make—the one that allows Bones the most play space? Which would be best for running? (Professional Standards for Teaching Mathematics, 1991, p. 28)

Discussions based on problems like these encourage students to explain their answers, tell how they arrived at their answers, justify their reasoning, and question other students.

Try this problem out on some friends. You'll have fun trying to convince the others that Bones will be better off with your plan than theirs. And you will be surprised at the inventive ways your friends go about solving the problem.

> "When students make public conjectures and reason with others about mathematics, ideas and knowledge are developed collaboratively, revealing mathematics as constructed by human beings within an intellectual community."
>
> – Professional Standards for Teaching Mathematics

Ways of Thinking in the Arts

I am limiting the focus on the arts to responding to music, visual art, and dance, since the studio aspects of these subjects are not within the scope of this book.

In many respects, the ways of thinking in the arts are like the ways of thinking in literature: experiencing, analyzing, and interpreting. Experts analyze why Mona Lisa's smile has haunted us for generations. Critics attempt to interpret the purpose of those splatters of paint from Jackson Pollock. I experience John Philip Sousa's *Stars and Stripes Forever* and look for a flag to wave. We respond to the arts, and exploring our responses through discussion enriches our lives.

GETTING DISCUSSION STARTED IN THE ARTS

Making personal connections with a work of dance, music, or visual art gets at the essence of human experience. Exploring those connections through discussion, comparing and contrasting viewpoints, promotes deeper understanding of the arts and their impact on us. For example, Jacques Brel's song *Old Folks* always clutches my heart:

The old folks don't talk much / And they talk so slowly when they do / They are rich, they are poor, their illusions are gone / They share one heart for two / Their homes all smell of thyme, of old photographs / And an old-fashioned song / Though you may live in town you live so far away / When you've lived too long / And have they laughed too much, do their dry voices crack / Talking of times gone by / And have they cried too much, a tear or two / Still always seems to cloud the eye / They tremble as they watch the old silver clock / When day is through / It tick-tocks oh so slow, it says, "Yes," it says, "No" / It says, "I'll wait for you." / The old folks dream no more / The books have gone to sleep, the piano's out of tune / The little cat is dead and no more do they sing / On a Sunday afternoon / The old folks move no more, their world's become too small / Their bodies feel like lead / They might look out the window or else sit in a chair / Or else they stay in bed / And if they still go out, arm in arm, arm in arm / In the morning's chill / It's to have a good cry, to say their last good-bye / To one who's older still / And then they go

> ## LISTENING IN
>
> Visit another teacher's classroom when content-area discussions are taking place. First, note if true discussion is occurring. Then note the similarities and differences between discussion in this classroom and that in your own.

home to the old silver clock / When day is through / It tick-tocks oh so slow, it says, "Yes," it says, "No" / It says, "I'll wait for you." / The old folks never die / They just put down their heads and go to sleep one day / They hold each other's hand like children in the dark / But one will get lost anyway / And the other will remain just sitting in that room / Which makes no sound / It doesn't matter now, the song has died away / And echoes all around / You'll see them when they walk through the sun-filled park / Where children run and play / It hurts too much to smile, it hurts too much but life goes on / For still another day / As they try to escape the old silver clock / When day is through / It tick-tocks oh so slow, it says, "Yes," it says, "No" / It says, "I'll wait for you." / The old, old silver clock that's hanging on the wall / That waits for us / All

The metronomic monotony of the tune adds to the poignancy of the words. Those of us who have had parents in nursing homes have much to discuss about this song.

Here are some guidelines for sparking discussion about the arts:

◆ **Explore responses deeply.** As with a piece of literature, understanding and expressing one's feelings about a work of art is critical. Why does one student soar with Mozart and another find his music saccharine? Why do some students find Salvador Dalí's painting disturbing and others revel in its iconoclasm and inventiveness? How is it that Merce Cunningham's choreography inspires some and

> What the painting makes me think of
>
> The painting makes me think of a relaxing Saturday picnic under the trees. I think that it is trying to show the beauty that a day can bring. I also think that the lake is showing the beauty of the land that is not seen in the picture. I think that the girl sitting by herself represents how to find peace is to find it in yourself and in a special place but not to necassarily find it with other people. I think that the whole painting is really about the joy of beauty and the beauty of peace. In many things one step leads to another and than finally to a conclusion and I think that is shown in the painting. I do find something that seems like a subtle hint is that the girl is alone so she has paddled in the boat and does not need a man to do that for her so in that small way it seems to be showing women are equal to men.

FIGURE 2-9: Nina writes a fully formed essay in her journal to prepare for a discussion of Monet's painting *The River*.

Classroom Discussion

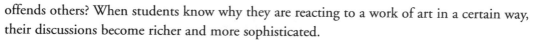

offends others? When students know why they are reacting to a work of art in a certain way, their discussions become richer and more sophisticated.

◆ **Delve into the artist's craft and use of elements.** Dance, music, and visual works are carefully crafted, and the elements are worth studying. Discussion of those elements can lead to a deeper understanding of how the artist creates a work of art. Students may explore the representation of light in the paintings of Rembrandt, the variations of a refrain in the music of Copland, or the way Martha Graham used gravity in her choreography.

◆ **Consider the cultural and contextual influences.** Fruitful discussion can center on the contextual and cultural influences that may have impacted the work. How interesting to discover the reason for all those Moorish influences on Spanish architecture of the eighth through twelfth centuries. How fascinating to learn about the patronage system of Mozart's time and its impact on his music. And vice versa: Rather than looking at the impact of context and culture on art, you can reverse the mirror and look at the impact of art on context and culture, such as Hitler's love of Wagner.

Figures 2-9 and 2-10 show journal entries from two middle-school students responding to the prompt "What does Monet's *The River* make you think of?" Nina's journal entry is in paragraph form, whereas Ray chose to make notes to himself. Both entries show a high level of thinking and an understanding that art is supposed to invite a deep, personal response.

> What The Painting makes me think of
> - a calm peaceful place.
> - getting away from all the hub-bub or noise.
> - thinking of floating in a boat.
> - trees and wildflowers.
> - being enchanted by the lovely scene.
> - wishing to just blend in.
> - wanting to become one with your setting, emotions, and feelings.
> - letting your feelings just rest.
> - soaring high in the sky.
> - being alone.
> - wondering, pondering.
> - getting away from everyday life.
> - thinking if this is what you really want.
> - wondering if there is a better life.
> - thinking over a problem.
> - maybe feeling too different from the rest of the people.
> - wishing to be somewhere else.
> - wanting something different than you already have.
> - yearning, craving, needing something.
> - gazing at the river mesmerized by it.

FIGURE 2-10: Ray prepares for the discussion by making notes rather than writing an essay, as Nina did. Both strategies are effective.

Using Response Journals to Prepare for Discussion

Response journals are typically used in literature discussion as a place for students to write down their thoughts about a book before meeting to talk about it. But they can be used for art discussions as well. Have students freewrite about a work of art or an art-related topic, or give them a prompt such as "How does this work make you feel?" or "If you could ask the choreographer or lead dancer one question, what would it be and why would you ask that question?" The written responses then become the basis for discussion.

Response journals have several functions:

◆ They give students the time (and the responsibility) to consider their response. Students reflect before they respond, which makes for a much richer discussion.

◆ They allow all students to come to the discussion with something to say, including those who are reticent and those who do not think quickly on their feet.

◆ They provide a place for discussion to begin and a place to return to if discussion bogs down.

◆ They provide an ongoing, permanent record of students' growth in the content area.

◆

Final Thought

Discussion is a wonderful tool for enhancing learning and thinking in all the content areas. It can be used to engage students, prepare them for learning, and aid them in the review and synthesis of ideas. But the development of discussion skills takes time, and you must be willing to invest that time. It will be well spent because your students will be learning the content of their curriculum while they polish their skills at discussion.

I hope that you are convinced of the value of including discussion in your classroom. In the remaining chapters, I look at exactly how to do that. Chapter 3 explores how to prepare for discussion in a variety of ways so that when your students engage in discussion, they will be successful.

Chapter Three

Preparing for Discussion: Setting Up for Success

Sometimes fruitful discussion simply springs forth all by itself, but don't count on it! Effective teachers spend a great deal of time preparing for discussion, which includes developing a classroom climate that welcomes and facilitates discussion, deciding whether whole-class or small-group discussion is the better format at a particular time for a particular goal, having transition strategies for moving students from whole-class to small-group discussion, and thinking carefully about the composition of the small groups. Preparation involves selecting engaging topics for discussion and ensuring that students will come to the discussion with something to say. Rules for discussion need to be developed. Successful discussions are the result of thoughtful, proactive planning and careful pacing throughout the year, week, and day. This chapter presents ways to achieve that.

Preparing the Classroom Climate for Discussion

The best discussions take place where there is a spirit of inquiry and an environment of trust.

Creating a Spirit of Inquiry

For discussion to be engaging and, in the end, transformative, students must be ready to take risks and explore the unknown, gaining new insights and understandings. Teaching that revolves around the IRE pattern (interrogation/response/evaluation) squelches this spirit and creates compliant students who don't take risks for fear of being wrong, who believe there is only one right answer (and hope to offer that answer before anyone else), and who expect the teacher to decide who is right. What an ugly picture! (See Chapter 1 for more information on the IRE pattern.) For discussion to flourish, students and teacher need to explore, to voyage out together into the unknown. Toward that end, Leslie Trowbridge, Rodger Bybee, and Janet Powell (2000) recommend that we introduce discussion with a positive attitude, one that says, "Together we are going to wrestle with some ideas, and it will be fun!"

Creating an Environment of Trust

As enjoyable as true discussion can be, it is complex and fraught with traps. The group has to grapple with issues of leadership, such as who will assume leadership and when and how leadership will be relinquished. The group has to resolve issues of participation, including the silencing and privileging of certain individuals. Participants must interact in ways that facilitate collaboration and a fair distribution of responsibility so that everyone has the opportunity to contribute by sharing their ideas and by listening. For all this to happen, there must be an environment of trust in the classroom.

I identified four kinds of trust that are necessary for productive discussion (1996):

◆ the teacher's trust of students
◆ the students' trust of the teacher
◆ the trust of one's peers
◆ the trust of oneself

The teacher must trust that the students can share control with her and manage their own discussions. She must also trust that the students will have something to say and can identify important

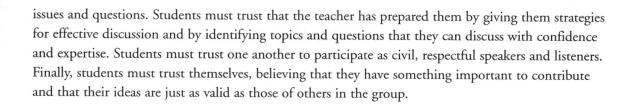

issues and questions. Students must trust that the teacher has prepared them by giving them strategies for effective discussion and by identifying topics and questions that they can discuss with confidence and expertise. Students must trust one another to participate as civil, respectful speakers and listeners. Finally, students must trust themselves, believing that they have something important to contribute and that their ideas are just as valid as those of others in the group.

Making Decisions About Groups and Grouping

Two main decisions need to be made about groups and grouping for discussion. The first is whether to group at all. Often small groups are perfect for discussion, but not always. Sometimes whole-class discussion makes more sense. Your decision should be based on the purposes of the discussion and on the degree to which the students are ready to work in small groups. If small groups are your choice, then move on to the second decision, which revolves around group membership. How will you divide the class into sets of students who can work productively together?

When Whole-Class Discussion Is Appropriate

Whole-class discussion can be effective and efficient for three main purposes: to provide guidance before students explore a new topic, to follow up after students have explored a new topic, and to give students models and opportunities to practice discussion.

WHOLE-CLASS DISCUSSION PROVIDES GUIDANCE BEFORE EXPLORING A NEW TOPIC

When presenting a new topic to students, we need to prepare them by determining background knowledge, building vocabulary, and setting purposes for learning. This can be accomplished through whole-class discussion.

Determining Background Knowledge

What do the students know about a topic? What do they need to know about it before they start in on a unit, a project, or a series of small-group discussions? As every experienced teacher knows, background knowledge can vary widely from class to class. Wise teachers routinely identify the

Background Knowledge Quiz

This activity helps you determine what your students already know about a topic and then think about your expectations.

1. Before exploring a topic with students, write down facts you expect them to know already. For example, before a study of minerals, you may expect the students to know that rocks are not alive, that there are many different kinds of rocks, and that rocks are made up of minerals.

2. Turn some of the facts into false statements and list them on a reproducible sheet, being careful that they are not patently untrue, like "Rocks are made of cheese" or "There is only one kind of rock." You might also include some common misconceptions about the topic, such as "Rocks are not useful." (See Figure 3-1 for a health education example.)

3. Distribute the sheet and have students mark each statement as true or false.

4. Engage the students in a discussion of their responses, making notes of additional information they seem to know and not know.

5. Use this information to plan your instruction. You now know what you don't need to teach and what you do.

Of course, the best time to give a background knowledge test is at least a couple of days before you start your unit. Then you can plan accordingly, introducing information the students do not have and bypassing background knowledge they already possess.

Background Knowledge Quiz

Mark each statement as true (T) or false (F). Be sure I can tell your T's from your F's!

_____ In general you should avoid most carbohydrates if you want to be healthy.

_____ A healthful diet includes some fat each day.

_____ Peanut butter is of little nutritional value. It's basically junk food.

_____ Whole-wheat bread is better for you than white bread.

_____ The best way to lose weight is to skip one meal a day.

_____ Low-fat foods are often high in sugar.

_____ You should have at least 8 ounces of protein every day.

_____ Cheese is about 60% fat.

_____ Adding 4 tablespoons of dressing to a salad adds about 250 calories.

FIGURE 3-1

List-Group-Label

Hilda Taba (1967) developed List-Group-Label as a vocabulary activity, but it can also be used to gain a sense of your class's background knowledge.

1. Ask students to tell you words related to a topic, such as the Renaissance. As students suggest words, write them on the board. If a word seems totally unrelated, such as *submarines*, include it only if the student can provide a rationale. Generally, you should accept all words. Once you have 15 to 25 words, move to the next step. (See Figure 3-2.)

2. Have pairs of students sort the words into categories. Each category should contain at least three words, although sometimes that won't be possible because words just don't fit together or students may not have the conceptual knowledge to sort them precisely. Once pairs have finished sorting, have them label their categories.

3. In a whole-class discussion, have pairs share their work, telling how they sorted and labeled words, and why. Use differences in approaches and labels to discuss the words and the ideas they represent.

4. Use the results of this activity to gain a sense of the background knowledge of the class. For example, Rose and Julio seem to know a lot about the Renaissance; Cicely and Andrew seem to know less, based on their grouping and labeling.

List-Group-Label

Our Class List

sculpture   Italy   Michelangelo   Renaissance man   1600s
classical influence   Middle Ages   cathedrals   Donatello
Botticelli   Florence   Leonardo da Vinci   genius
Raphael   Mona Lisa   Sistine Chapel   Piéta
painting

Rose and Julio's List

What About
painting
sculpture
cathedrals
Ren. man
classical influence
genius

Famous Works
Mona Lisa
Sistine Chapel
Piéta

When and Where
Italy   1600s
Florence
(after) the Middle Ages

Famous People
Michelangelo
Donatello
da Vinci
Raphael

Cicely and Andrew's List

Art
painting
sculpture
Mona Lisa
Renaissance man

Time and Place
Italy   1600s
Middle Ages
Cathedrals
Sistine Chapel
Classical influence

genius ??

Artists
Michelangelo
Donatello
Florence
Botticelli
Raphael
Piéta
Leonardo da V.

FIGURE 3-2

knowledge they assume students already have about a new topic. Introductory whole-class discussion can reveal the depth of student knowledge about a topic and any gaps in that knowledge that need to be filled. It also makes students aware that they already know something about the topic and so may give them confidence. Later in the chapter, I discuss how to help students activate their background knowledge so that they arrive at discussions prepared.

Building Vocabulary

Whole-class discussion can ensure that each student begins a unit, project, or series of small-group discussions with at least a basic understanding of the critical vocabulary. Of course, you'll want to discuss unfamiliar terms as they arise, but it's also a good idea to preteach words necessary to understanding the topic that students will investigate. This gets them off to a good start.

To help you think about your students' existing vocabularies, fill in a chart like the one shown in Figure 3-3. (You'll find a blank version in Appendix 4.) Most likely, your students will be able to read some words and understand completely what they mean. Other words and phrases, however, may give them trouble; students will recognize them but at best only vaguely understand them. (Take *sardonic*, *puce*, and *parathyroid gland*, for example. You probably recognize those words and can even pronounce them correctly, but do you know what they mean?) Then there are words that you do not expect your students to know at all. Most likely, these words represent the new concepts that you will introduce in the unit, project, or series of small-group discussions you plan to launch.

You can use the same chart with the students. Have them rate their own under-

Vocabulary Expectations Chart

Word	Recognize and have meaning	Have word recognition	Won't know at all
atom	X		
radioactive		X	
gamma rays			X
isotopes			X
fission/fusion		X	
critical mass		X	
half-life			X

FIGURE 3-3: Use this chart to help you decide on words to focus on when preparing students for a new unit. You can fill it out based on your knowledge of the class or have students fill it out themselves.

ACTIVITY

Exclusion Brainstorming

Camille Blachowicz (1986) designed Exclusion Brainstorming to help students discover what they already know about a topic. This activity has more teacher control than List-Group-Label because you prepare the list of words for the students rather than taking suggestions from them.

1. Develop a list of about 15 words related to a topic you are about to cover, in order to get a sense of your class's existing vocabulary. Choose five words directly related to the topic, five completely unrelated to the topic, and five ambiguous ones. If you were about to embark on a unit titled "The Orchestra," you could choose:

woodwinds	solo	synthesizer	piano
Mick Jagger	chair	soprano	reeds
timpani	tenor	conductor	viola
banjo	harp	electric guitar	

2. Ask students to identify the words they think do not relate to the topic and explain their reasoning. Encourage them to challenge one another respectfully and seek clarification.
3. From the remaining list, have students select words they predict are related to the orchestra and tell why, again challenging one another and seeking clarification.
4. Have students discuss the remaining words (which will most likely be ambiguous), telling what they think the words mean and how they may be related to the orchestra.

standing of the key words. Then engage them in a discussion of the meanings of the words they think they know and introduce them to the words they don't know.

Many activities designed to build background knowledge can be adapted to teach topic-specific vocabulary, including List-Group-Label (Figure 3-2) and Exclusion Brainstorming, which is described above. (See Chapter 2 for more on using discussion to prepare students for reading, viewing, and listening.)

Setting Purposes for Learning

In whole-class discussion, students can work collaboratively with you to identify important purposes for a unit, project, or series of small-group discussions. For example, some fourth graders are apt to be quite interested in studying Native Americans who lived in their state before the arrival of

Expectation Outline

The Expectation Outline helps students set purposes for learning and provides a guide for reading (Spiegel, 1981). Students think about information they expect to find in their reading, viewing, or listening, and then organize that information into higher-level concepts.

1. Ask students what information they expect a good author to provide about a topic, such as animals. Write their responses on the board, grouping related ones, but without comment. For example, students may offer, "How many legs it has" and "How long it lives." If the responses fall into different categories, write them in different spots on the board, *but do not label them*. You might place the third response, "What color it is," next to "How many legs . . ." to begin to create the implicit category What It Looks Like. Later, you may place a response such as "How it has babies" near "How long it lives" as part of the Life Cycle category.

2. When the students seem to have run out of suggestions, point to the first cluster of information. Ask students to make up a title for it. Do this for all clusters. (See Figure 3-4.)

3. Review the clusters and ask if anyone has additional expectations. As students respond, ask them to tell you under which category a new expectation should be placed. I always introduce an additional category: Two Bizarre Facts I Never Expected. Students love this one because there are always interesting tidbits that don't fit into any category but are fun to learn. (Did you know that when tarantulas are threatened, they rear up on their back legs and mew like a cat?)

Tell students to use the Expectation Outline to guide their reading. Challenge them to see how many of their expectations the author really did meet. At the same time, inform them that no author will provide every piece of information they expect. It is particularly effective to have different groups of students read different texts about the same topic and pool their information.

Expectation Outline: Animals

What It Looks Like
how many legs
what color
weight
body covering
how tall

Life Cycle
how long does it live
how does it have babies
how many babies at a time
mate for life?

Habits
what does it eat
how does it move
diurnal? nocturnal?
noises it makes
how catch/get what it eats

Habitat
what eats it
where does it live
— country
— climate
— air? water? land?
does it have a "home" (nest, cave)

FIGURE 3-4

K-W-L Strategy

Donna Ogle's K-W-L strategy (1986) is an excellent way to introduce a topic to the whole class. Like the Expectation Outline, it addresses three important aspects of preparation: background knowledge, vocabulary, and purpose.

1. Ask students to tell you what they already know about the topic (K) and what they want to know about it (W). Record their responses on a large chart like the one shown in Figure 3-5. Be sure to keep this chart posted in the classroom so that you can use it again later. The K step allows you to assess the level of the class's background knowledge (and fill in gaps as needed), and the W step helps the class set goals. These steps also allow you to assess vocabulary knowledge, to see what terms the students associate with the topic, and to question them about their understanding of the terms.

2. If a student challenges a "known fact" in the K column, turn the fact into a question and place it in the second column. This encourages students to get into the habit of checking uncertain information for accuracy.

3. Post the chart in a prominent place as the class studies the topic. As a culminating activity, ask the class to tell you what they have learned through their exploration (L). Record their answers in the chart's last column. In the W column, place new information next to related information so students can see that they've fulfilled some of the goals they set.

4. If information in the L column contradicts information in the K column, cross out the incorrect information in the K column. Be sure students understand that good readers often find out that what they "know" is wrong and that finding errors is a mark of successful reading.

K-W-L Chart: The Korean War

Know	Want to Know	Learned
in Korea lots of injuries 1950's ?	How did we get into the war How many killed	UN action 25,000 1950s
fighting over some line	what parallel	38th parallel
helicopters	How did it end	truce; Korea divided
Japan~~se~~=bad guys	Who = bad guys?	N.Korea China
*M*A*S*H reruns		

FIGURE 3-5

Europeans—tribal ceremonies, warfare with the settlers, famous leaders, food, government, and so on—whereas some students won't be interested in the subject at all! In a whole-class discussion, you could guide students to narrow the class's focus to two important goals, such as learning about the aspects of the Native American culture that the Europeans adopted and the role of Native Americans in the multicultural history of the state. In this way, those interested in everything don't go off on tangents and those interested in nothing know where to put their energies.

A simple planning chart, like the one shown in Figure 3-6, can help you prepare for a whole-class discussion that will introduce a new topic. (See Appendix 5 for a reproducible version of this chart.) Here are some questions to ask yourself as you fill out the chart:

Planning Chart for Whole-Class Discussion

Essential Background Knowledge
- Communities are not just people.
- We have an effect on our "community."
- There are endangered species
- "   "   "   habitats

Essential Vocabulary

already know	pre-teach	teach as we go
community	ecosystem	{abiotic (p.421)
food chain	{carnivore	{biotic
decompose	{herbivore	
carbon	{omnivore	nitrogen cycle
nitrogen	limiting factors	
photosynthesis		

Goals/Purposes

Why? – to know how to be responsible citizens to preserve the environment

Big ideas – ① ecosystems are very delicate
② "   "   " interdependent
③ We have an effect on our ecosystem

FIGURE 3-6

Essential Background Knowledge
1. What facts do I expect students to know before we start?
2. What big ideas do I expect them to know?

Essential Vocabulary
1. What words/terms do I expect them to know already?
2. What words/terms will I teach them before we start?
3. What words/terms will I teach them during the unit?

U-Debate Forum

U-Debates (Athanases, 1998) are helpful when you are addressing a topic that invites a difference of opinion, such as "Should we retain the Electoral College?," "Which is more critical, preserving the rain forest for ecological reasons or allowing it to be harvested for economic reasons?," or "Was Goldilocks wrong to eat the porridge at the Three Bears' house?"

1. Arrange all seats in the classroom into a U shape. The seats on the left side of the U are designated for the students who hold View A; the seats on the right side are for those who hold View B; and the seats on the curve are for those who hold a neutral view or are undecided.

2. Ask the students to take seats corresponding to their views. Within a group, students may even order themselves according to the strength of their views. The first seat on Side A may represent the most adamant proponent. This may take some negotiation if two or more students hold especially strong viewpoints, but be sure students don't dwell on exact seating. Make the decision for them, if necessary.

3. Have a discussion. Because students know from the seating who is likely to support or challenge them, they can direct their comments appropriately, appealing to those who share their view or addressing a concern to those who do not. As their views change, encourage students to move to different seats.

Goals/Purposes

1. Why do the students need to know this information?
2. What big ideas do I want them to understand by the end of the unit?

WHOLE-CLASS DISCUSSION PROVIDES FOLLOW-UP AFTER STUDENTS HAVE EXPLORED A NEW TOPIC

Whole-class discussion at the culmination of a unit, project, or series of small-group discussions has two important functions. First, it is a natural way to review important concepts to ensure students understand them. Whole-class discussion is especially useful for bringing the class back together to share new knowledge and merge small pieces of information into big ideas. In a unit on the human body, for example, small groups can explore the digestive, respiratory, circulatory, excretory, endocrine, nervous, reproductive, skeletal, and muscular systems. In the follow-up whole-class discussion, students then develop two important general concepts: Each system has a special function, and all systems need to work together to keep the body functioning efficiently. The discussion provides an opportunity to learn what others have found out, to clarify concepts, and to lodge important ideas in long-term memory. Students leave the unit with the big picture, not just knowledge of one small part or a collection of interesting facts that don't add up to anything.

Second, whole-class discussion is a way for you to assess if the goals for the unit, project, or series of discussions have been reached. It tells you what the students understand and still don't understand, and then you can reteach as necessary.

WHOLE-CLASS DISCUSSION SHOWS STUDENTS WHAT AND HOW TO DISCUSS

Chances are, whole-class and small-group discussions will fail if students do not know what to discuss and how to discuss. They may know how to converse and to report, but they often lack the strategies necessary for true discussion. (In Chapter 4, I describe these strategies in detail.) Whole-class discussion is the perfect forum for introducing these strategies because it allows students both to observe you modeling them and to practice them under your guidance.

What to Discuss

In a true discussion, all participants ask questions, not just the teacher. In whole-group discussion, you can show students how to ask effective questions in a variety of ways. One way is through modeling "good" and "bad" questions. (My father always said, "A bad example is just as good as a good example, as long as you know the difference.") In a discussion of obesity, for example, you might pose good questions, such as "What are the dangers to one's health from obesity?" and "How can we encourage someone we love to lose weight?" After that, you might pose bad questions, such as "How many calories are in a cheeseburger?" and "What is the definition of obesity in our health book?" Explain why the "good" questions are good and the "bad" ones are bad, then lead students in developing a class chart that describes good and bad initiating questions.

Let's see how good and bad initiating questions work in a whole-class discussion of *Terrible Things* (Bunting, 1993), which describes how evil, predatory creatures take away species of animals from the forest, one by one. It is a powerful allegory for the Holocaust.

> **Good Initiating Questions**
> - do not have one right answer,
> - focus on a big idea not a little detail,
> - lead to other questions.
>
> **Bad Initiating Questions**
> - have a right answer, so there is nothing to discuss,
> - focus on only a small part of the picture,
> - don't go anywhere.

TEACHER: Who wants to start our discussion with a good question?

BECKY: Who were the first animals taken?

SAM: The birds.

[The teacher allows the silence to build for a bit.]

TEACHER: I think that question didn't really get us started because there wasn't anything to discuss. It had a right answer, and Sam knew what it was. Does anyone have a question that might get us started because it doesn't have one right answer?

FRANCISCO: Why were the Terrible Things so mean?

MARY ANN: Because they were evil.

JAAP: Because they didn't like anything that wasn't like them.

BILLY: But we don't know what the Terrible Things were like. They are just blurry shapes in the book.

JAAP: Yeah, but we are pretty sure they weren't little animals like the ones in the forest.

MILDRED: I want to know why the animals didn't stick up for each other. As long as the Terrible Things weren't after them, like the bunnies, no one tried to stop them.

CINDY: That was awful. I'd stick up for my friends.

MILDRED: But what if they weren't really your friends? I mean, no one particularly liked the frogs, so they just let the Terrible Things take them. Should you only stick up for your friends?

OLAF: Well, I wouldn't stick my neck out for someone I didn't like. What if they went after me?

MILDRED: And see what happened. The Terrible Things got everyone in the end.

Note how Francisco's question generates a bit of discussion because it doesn't have one clear answer. It leads to the important concept that the Terrible Things, like the Nazis, exterminated anyone who was not like them. Mildred's question provokes even more discussion because it leads to other questions and focuses on the central theme of the book.

How to Discuss

In our work with fifth graders, my colleagues and I (Day, Spiegel, McLellan, & Brown, 2002) found that students tended to "round-robin" report rather than discuss: They came to their small groups prepared to say something but paid little attention to what others said. We also found some students lacked socially appropriate ways to disagree. In other words, they tended to be critical and disrespectful toward participants who didn't share their viewpoints.

Teacher modeling during whole-class discussions can help prevent such problems. You can model how to follow up on a comment with another ("What made you think that?" or "I'm not convinced yet. Say some more about that") and how to disagree politely ("That's not how I interpreted that. I think . . ." or "Wow! I came up with an entirely different conclusion that . . ."). Whatever you do, be sure to resist modeling the IRE pattern of discussion, which places the focus on a leader who looks for one right response and then evaluates it. It is a guaranteed discussion-killer. (For more information on the IRE pattern, see Chapter 1. For more information on facilitating discussion, see Chapter 4.)

When Small-Group Discussion Is Appropriate

Just as whole-class discussion has its own purposes, so does small-group discussion. Small-group discussion is ideal for helping students make meaning, take responsibility for learning, and practice effective strategies.

SMALL-GROUP DISCUSSION HELPS STUDENTS MAKE MEANING

The construction of meaning—making sense of information, "putting it all together" to form new ideas—is central to learning. When students work alone, of course, they can make meaning, often powerful meaning. But as we've seen, discussion provides opportunities for reflection and revision of meaning, opportunities that are less likely to occur when working alone. Further, sharing their thoughts forces students to be explicit in their thinking so they can present their ideas clearly. And listening to the meaning others construct may lead to conflict from which new ideas may emerge. Through social interaction, meaning is likely to be richer and more thoughtfully constructed (Almasi, 1995).

Because small-group discussion has fewer participants than whole-class discussion, the quality of interactions is likely to be better and more suitable for meaning making. Individual voices are apt to be heard because there is less competition for "airtime." Students listen more carefully in a small group because it is easier to hear and harder to avoid paying attention. Students are more likely to engage in the discussion because the context is more personal. The group may stay more focused because there are fewer people to move the discussion off track.

SMALL-GROUP DISCUSSION HELPS STUDENTS TAKE RESPONSIBILITY FOR LEARNING

In small-group discussions, everyone needs to contribute. It is hard to shirk one's responsibilities in a small group. Donna Alvermann and her colleagues (1996) found that middle school students are well aware of what makes a small-group discussion successful: sharing

> "I think the smaller group was better because there are less people to hassle us. You can go ahead and say something that you're not real sure about. Try out ideas."
>
> – Middle school student in an interview conducted by Donna Alvermann and her colleagues for a study on discussion in the content areas

the responsibility of initiating and maintaining discussion, recognizing individual responsibility to contribute pertinent information, and sharing personal beliefs. They also understand the importance of involving all group members and know how to do that, how to keep order, and how to stay focused. Indeed, each participant must shoulder their fair share of the work.

> "Small group discussions seemed to promote students' class involvement by increasing the number of times they could talk and by decreasing risks they took when expressing personal and tentative thoughts."
>
> – Donna Alvermann and her colleagues

SMALL-GROUP DISCUSSION HELPS STUDENTS PRACTICE EFFECTIVE STRATEGIES

Because students are more likely to speak up and stay engaged in small groups, which are less formal and "more real" than teacher-led whole-class discussion, they are a better setting for practicing discussion strategies, such as inviting others to participate, asking follow-up questions, and providing clarification. Also, because students typically lead small-group discussions, they begin to develop independence in managing those discussions. (See Chapter 4 for more information on student facilitation of discussion.)

Considerations for Selecting Small Group Members

For discussions that last for only one or two meetings, arbitrary grouping is fine. Students can count off by fives or draw group assignments from a hat. But for extended discussions, the composition of the groups is crucial and requires careful arrangement. This is no easy task! Among the factors you need to consider are group size, each student's position and status within the classroom, friendships, personality traits, gender relationships, and reading abilities.

There are no clear-cut rules for selecting members of small groups, but here are two rules of thumb:

◆ **Be flexible.** Change group membership often throughout the year. A group that isn't working can be split up; a student who suddenly becomes reticent can be paired with a supportive friend; a student who has an intellectual growth spurt can be placed in a more advanced group.

◆ **Assess regularly.** Visit each group on an ongoing basis to determine how well it is working and to identify any barriers to success. (See the box on page 72 and Chapter 6 for more information on assessing discussions.)

Who decides group membership? In many instances you do, especially at the beginning of a school year. However, as the year proceeds, you may consult the class. As students become more responsible and familiar with their classmates, don't be surprised if they also develop the skills necessary to choose their groups independently. For more ideas on forming groups, see *Great Grouping Strategies* by Ronit M. Wrubel (2002).

GROUP SIZE

Karen Allan and Margery Miller (2000) suggest forming groups of about five students, which allows everyone a chance to talk and provides enough different points of view to create the need for discussion. My colleagues and I (Day et al., 2002) found that groups of

---

Three Steps to Assessing a Group's Success

◆ Determine levels of participation. Be alert to sudden drops or changes in students' contributions.
◆ Determine what might be barriers to participation, such as text difficulty, grouping issues, or insufficient discussion skills.
◆ Determine the level at which the problem is occurring (whole class, small group, or individual student) and the form of intervention required (strategy lessons, modeling, or direct intervention).

ACTIVITY

Consult the Class

Once the students know each other well and understand what it takes to form an effective discussion group, involve them in forming the small groups.

1. Ask students to list confidentially the seven classmates they would most like to be in a group with, as well as up to three they would prefer *not* to work with. Stress the importance of confidentiality and the risk of hurting feelings if the lists are shared; it is absolutely forbidden for students to share their lists with anyone but you.

2. Use the information to form small groups, which is not as easy as it sounds. Sometimes students will make poor choices that you simply cannot honor. Remember that your job is to create the most effective groups possible given the variety of students that you have, not to make students happy by honoring all their requests. In addition, you will almost always find it easy to form most of the groups only to find that you have to revise your plan in order to place the last three members of the class appropriately. Finding a good place for an aggressive or particularly reticent student may mean reshuffling the membership of several other groups you thought were already formed.

3. Be sure students understand that they are consultants and that the final decision is yours.

this size worked well for fifth-grade students. (See our assessment guide in box on page 72.) So strive for groups of four to six, perhaps going with fewer members when quick agreement is expected and discussion will be brief, ensuring that everyone has a chance to contribute. With groups of more than six, you run the risk of some students' being silenced because too many students are trying to be heard.

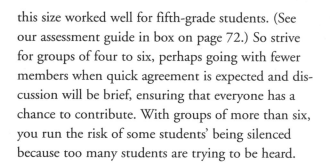

LISTENING IN

Try out groups of different sizes. See if you can identify an optimal size for your class, based on all the grouping considerations discussed in this section.

POSITION AND STATUS WITHIN THE CLASSROOM

Positioning theory looks at how we develop a sense of self in relation to others—how we position ourselves in social interactions and how others position us (Davies & Harré, 1990). An individual may have a position as an Insider—a person whose opinion is valued—in one setting but as an Outsider in another. Outsiders find classrooms risky places to be because they feel their voices are silenced and their ideas are not viewed as important. In consequence, they behave problematically, being disruptive, uncooperative, and argumentative. Some Outsiders even strike preemptively: Knowing they are not welcome in a group,

ACTIVITY

Pick Your Spot

Try this activity when you want students to divide themselves into groups whose members have similar opinions for one or two discussions.

1. Identify a question that has several possible answers or perspectives. Ask each student to select one perspective from your list in order to write a persuasive essay. For example, you may ask, "Who was the most influential post-impressionist painter, Cézanne, Van Gogh, or Gauguin?" or "What is the best way to encourage recycling in our community: curbside service, payment for recyclable materials, or fines for failure to recycle?"

2. For each perspective, name a location in the room and tell the students who have selected that perspective to gather there—the Cézanne group near the door, the Van Gogh group at the front, and the Gauguin supporters near the windows.

3. Each group discusses the perspective they have chosen, sharing their rationale and pooling their knowledge. They don't have to waste time persuading each other of the merit of their choice but can get right to the business of persuading others (Ellis & Whalen, 1990).

they misbehave and force their removal from the group. A wise teacher keeps an eye on how different students are positioned within the classroom and takes this into account when forming small groups.

Status is related to position. Students are "assigned" status by their classmates for a variety of reasons, including perceived or actual academic competence, race, gender, and socioeconomic status. Then that status becomes a substitute for actual performance. Thus, low-status students are categorized as unable to contribute to the group, based not on performance but solely on what their classmates expect of them because of that status. Watch what happens when Shannon, a low-status struggling reader, makes an insightful comment in this group of higher-achieving girls:

CAROLYN: I kind of felt alone sometimes just because, like my family would make decisions and they wouldn't, like, let me in on them, like with the cat's name.

KATE: Well, that's different from Carlie or Joey [characters in *The Pinballs* who are in foster care].

SHANNON: But they're not really family. They're like close friends. They're not really family, you know, by law, but—

KATE: *[interrupting]* Sharice, would you like to go?

Shannon is simply ignored, even though her comment could lead to an interesting discussion of the definition of family, a central theme of the book. Clearly, careful formation of groups is needed to prevent the all too typical pecking order from hindering the discussion.

FRIENDSHIPS

We all like to be in discussion groups with friends, and students are no exception. Surprisingly, however, Donna Alvermann and her colleagues (1996) found that as the school year progressed and middle school students became familiar with all their classmates, productivity and personality traits became more important than friendships. Thus, even though Tonita and Ann are best friends, Tonita may not want to work in a group with Ann because she knows Ann doesn't do her fair share. So consider placing friends together to some degree at the beginning of the year, when students are still learning how to discuss. That way the group can concentrate on developing discussion skills and completing their task, and not have to work too much on getting along with each other. Then, as skills develop, separate friends as you see fit and assess the impact on learning.

PERSONALITY TRAITS

Ideally, all students would get along with one another, but in reality almost every classroom has a few students who seem to have trouble getting along with anyone! There are also students who are extremely reticent or lack confidence or can't get along with others. What do you do with those students?

There are as many solutions as there are personalities, and sometimes they work and sometimes they don't. Placing challenging students in the setting that has the most potential for success requires a great deal of thought, a lot of hope, and a willingness to intervene as needed. Pairing students with complementary personality traits may help. For example, you could pair an extremely bossy student with a patient, diplomatic student who can help "tone down" the bossy student with comments such as "Let's see what Juan thinks" or "You pretty much made the last decision by yourself. Let's have the group vote on this one."

However, such pairings are not always successful. My colleagues and I (Day et al., 2002) report that when a reticent girl, Sharice, was paired with a more outspoken friend, Tanya, for literature circles, the strategy backfired. The hope was that Tanya would encourage Sharice to speak up and include her in discussions. However, Tanya was so anxious for Sharice to succeed that she spoke for her, thus making it unnecessary for Sharice to speak at all!

Even though complementary pairing is not always successful, it is worth trying. It can offer temporary support until the challenging student can work successfully in small groups. It also allows you to sprinkle the more difficult-to-place students around and, therefore, diffuse potential disruptions.

Avoid forming an entire group with Outsiders or students who have trouble working in groups. Such isolation provides these students with no role models or support for changing their behavior and makes you complicit in the continuation of their Outsider status.

GENDER RELATIONSHIPS

A number of researchers have investigated the role of gender in discussion. Laura Billings and Jill Fitzgerald (2002) summarized such investigations, indicating that, in general, males tend to talk, challenge, and interrupt more than females. Females ask more questions and tend to encourage other participants to respond. So one potential danger in mixed-gender groups is that the males might silence the females. One solution, of course, is to have only single-gender groups. Some would argue, though, that single-gender groups don't solve the problem but only avoid it. A better solution may be conducting frank, whole-class discussion about the pitfalls of mixed-gender groups to build awareness of and prevent problematic behaviors before they happen in small-group discussions.

Assigning within-group tasks may also be helpful. For example, if girls are the only ones who are encouraging comments or seeking clarification, then give each boy in a group two prompter cards that require him to ask at least one follow-up question after a participant has made a response. You may also ask one of the boys to keep a tally of who talks so that he sees inequities firsthand. If there is a great deal of disparity between who talks and who doesn't, give each group member five "talk" tokens (these can be blank cards or chips or any other counting device). Group members must "spend" all five tokens, but no more than five, in a discussion. (See the discussion of Talk Tokens in Chapter 4.)

READING ABILITY

Reading ability usually comes into play when students are preparing to discuss, since often they must read something before coming to the group. A student who does not have the ability to gain the information that will form the basis of the discussion is in an untenable situation. This may be a student who is learning disabled, who is unable to speak English well enough to participate fully, or who is simply at a low level in reading. For example, Tanya, a fifth grader, participated in several literature discussion groups throughout the year. When the group picked a book Tanya could read, she participated fully and made insightful comments in group discussions. But when the group selected a book that was too hard for her, she was uncooperative and rude, attempting to mask her inability to participate in the discussion through unacceptable behavior. Apparently, Tanya believed that is was better to be thought of as uncooperative and rude than as someone who is unable to read well (Day et al., 2002).

There are two basic ways to solve this problem. One is to find an alternative way for struggling students to gain the information. They may listen to the reading assignment on tape or to you or another student reading it aloud. You could give the student an abridged version of the reading assignment. Or you could assign the reading far in advance so the student has enough time to finish it before the discussion.

The other solution is to modify the groups for some tasks, matching students with similar reading abilities and tailoring reading assignments accordingly. In modified groups, there is still a range of ability levels but the range is more restricted and the reading assignment is appropriate for the lower end of the range. For example, if reading ability for a sixth-grade classroom ranges from second to ninth grade, and

Forming Groups: Steps to Follow

1. Write each student's name on a small stick-on note or card.
2. Separate out "hard-to-place" students, since you need to consider them first, rather then trying to fit them in at the end.
3. Pair each hard-to-place student with a "facilitator," a student who can help the other succeed through coaching and other forms of support.
4. Disperse each hard-to-place/facilitator pair across the groups, with no more than two pairs in one group. (Hopefully, you won't have that many hard-to-place students!)
5. Fill in the groups, considering reading level first, if that is a factor for the assignment, then position and status, and then gender.
6. Look to see if each student has a friend in the group. If not, switch students around. However, do not compromise any of the other decisions you have made to do this; the other considerations are more important than friendship.

Classroom Discussion

the assigned reading is at the high second-grade level, Group A may be composed of students reading at the second- and third-grade level, Group B might be those students reading around the fourth-grade level, Group C those at grade level, and Group D those above grade level. These are temporary groups just for specific tasks. As students grow in their reading ability, the groups will change.

Whichever solution you choose, you run the danger of identifying some students as "poor readers." But don't kid yourself—the rest of the class already knows who the less able readers are. It is better to give struggling readers tasks at which they can be successful and move them slowly forward than to set them up to fail continuously.

Selecting Questions for Discussion

Donna Alvermann and her colleagues' (1996) middle school students reported that the quality of discussion was dependent on the quality of the question selected by the teacher. If a question was too hard, students lacked the background knowledge to have anything but a superficial discussion. If the question was too easy, students had little to discuss because usually there was an obvious answer. If the question was boring and unrelated to students' personal lives, they were not willing to put forth the effort to have a discussion.

Alvermann and her colleagues' students are quite typical, so it's important for us to listen to them. But at the same time, we must also consider curricular needs and objectives. Students may be

Selecting an Application-Level Question and Set of Prep Questions: Steps to Follow

1. **Identify a curricular goal.**
   Example: *The students will understand the importance of water as an economic resource that must be used wisely.*
2. **Write an application-level question based on that goal.**
   Example: *What can my family do to avoid water shortages in our community?*
3. **Write a set of Prep Questions.** This ensures that students have adequate background knowledge for discussing the application-level question.
   Example: *What are the sources of water in our community? How is water used by our families and the rest of our community? What are the causes of water shortages in our community?*

desperately interested in and have a lot of knowledge about Britney Spears's love life, but it is unlikely that a discussion question based on that will advance their knowledge of American history or earth science.

So the first step for selecting a question for discussion is to identify a curricular goal. The second step is to write a question based on that goal at the application level. Benjamin Bloom's taxonomy (1956) defines *application* as using a concept learned in the classroom in a new situation. An application question requires the students to synthesize information to solve a real problem. For example, if your class is studying different forms of energy, you could ask, "What do you predict will be the most common source of energy for providing power to homes by 2050?" Or if your students are working on ratios, you might pose the following problem: "Today we are going to make chocolate chip cookies in class. The recipe makes 36 cookies. We want to make 81 cookies so that everyone in our class of 26, plus me, can have 3 cookies. How will you figure out how much of each ingredient we need?" Application-level questions are ideal for discussion for two reasons: They are likely to engage students because they are related to their lives, and they generally are not easy to answer, which gives students something to discuss.

Once you've identified a curricular goal and come up with an application-level question based on it, prepare the students for discussion by giving them a set of Prep Questions, usually ones that ask for simple facts, ensuring that students have gathered and reviewed the information needed for a meaningful discussion. Prep Questions can be answered by students individually, in small groups, or as a whole class. Once Prep Questions have been answered, students will be better prepared for an application-level small-group discussion.

The following guidelines may help you identify whether or not you have selected a good application-level question:

1. Is the question related to the curriculum?
   ◆ Is it at the application level?
   ◆ What "big ideas" from the curriculum does the question lead to?
2. Is the question pitched at the right level?
   ◆ Is it too hard?
     • Do the students lack the necessary background knowledge?
     • Is the question too broad?
     • Will it take a great deal of time to discuss this question?

LISTENING IN

Get into the habit of making a note of topics that lead to spontaneous discussion in your classroom. Try to identify the characteristics of those topics and use the information when choosing topics and questions for more structured discussions.

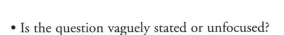

- Is the question vaguely stated or unfocused?
- Is anyone in the group likely to be unsuccessful in this discussion, even with appropriate effort?

◆ Is the question too easy?
- Is it a closed question, with one "right" answer?
- Is the question too narrow?
- Even if the question can be viewed from more than one perspective, will only one perspective likely be taken by the group?

3. Is the question engaging and interesting?
   ◆ Does it relate to the students' lives in some way?
   ◆ Does it focus on an important problem?
   ◆ Will students naturally bring different perspectives to the discussion?

DISCUSSION STIFLER

"We Can't Talk About That"

Controversial topics such as racism or capital punishment often make for lively discussions. Some teachers shy away from these topics because they are emotionally charged, but these are the very kinds of topics that young people need practice discussing because they give them experience offering logical, self-controlled arguments when faced with someone who disagrees passionately.

Here are some steps for introducing controversial topics for discussion:

◆ Learn your school's guidelines on covering controversial topics in the classroom and follow them.

◆ If the guidelines permit controversial topics, review the rules of discussion with your students, especially those that deal with ways of disagreeing civilly.

◆ Have students prepare more carefully than usual, writing their points out ahead of time and organizing their arguments.

◆ Structure the discussion a little more than usual, perhaps by putting a time limit on each speaker or on the number of times one person can speak. Schedule an ending time for the discussion and make it clear to everyone.

◆ Serve as a moderator to guide the discussion and, if need be, defuse and redirect it.

Ensuring Students Come to Small-Group Discussions Well Informed

It is our job to ensure that students have good questions to discuss in small groups. It is also our job to ensure that students are able to discuss those questions knowledgeably and appropriately. There are three ways to do that: by helping students mobilize and use their background knowledge, by having them write as preparation for discussion, and by giving them guidelines for carrying out rich, respectful discussions.

Mobilizing and Using Background Knowledge

We've seen that a good discussion question requires students to have a certain level of background knowledge. There are many ways for you to help students make this knowledge accessible, including making available books and magazines, the Internet, lectures, pictures and video, and other information sources. But there is also a less obvious and possibly more effective strategy: taking advantage of the range of background knowledge in your class. Rather than trying to be sure every student has the same knowledge, an impossible task, take advantage of the different things your students already know to enrich discussion.

When students use the same information sources, they come away with different types and levels of knowledge, depending on their interest in, experience with, and ability to learn about the topic. A student who is interested pays attention to new information and, as a result, gains background knowledge that a less-interested student doesn't even notice. For example, a student who is fascinated by infections and has gathered information on his own, outside of school, may become the class expert on staphylococcus. A student who has had personal experience with the death of a pet brings a different background to *The Tenth Good Thing About Barney* (Viorst, 1971) than a classmate who has never lost a pet. A student who is especially motivated, has a good memory, or, yes, learns easily may remember more of the information. Differences in background knowledge can be an asset to discussion as long as each student has something to contribute.

Writing as Preparation for Discussion

There's no better way to promote the richest possible discussion than by giving students adequate time to prepare for discussion through writing. But this means you have to give them the gift of time. Asking students to prepare for discussion on their own time (at home or at school during free time) won't work. They won't do it and they will be unprepared. Giving students the time to pre-

Putting It All Together

This grouping strategy uses differences in background knowledge to promote rich discussion. It is especially useful when reading abilities vary widely within one classroom.

1. Select four to five reading assignments on one topic that reflect the varying levels of reading ability in your classroom. This ensures all students will have a text they can read, and each group will have somewhat different information to bring to the discussion.

    Example: With a fifth-grade class studying tarantulas, you might have an article from *Ranger Rick* for your most challenged readers, a couple of sections from library books written at the fifth-grade level for your on-grade-level readers, and an article from a reliable Internet site, such as the National Wildlife Federation's KidZone, written at about the seventh-grade level for your most successful readers. All selections are about tarantulas, but each selection is at a different level and provides different information.

    Be sure that the easiest selections contain some interesting and unique information that the harder selections do not. Struggling readers should have sole access to some important information. In other words, the easiest selections must not be just watered-down versions of harder selections.

2. Follow the usual jigsaw grouping procedures:
    ◆ Divide the class into reading-ability groups. (Group A reads Selection A at the second-grade level; Group B reads Selection B at the fifth-grade level, and so on.)
    ◆ Have the students discuss what information will be important to share in subsequent discussions. This allows them to identify and clarify critical points and gives them confidence.
    ◆ Regroup so that each new group has one member from each of the original groups.
    ◆ Have the new groups continue discussing the topic, with each member sharing information that may be new to the other members. Discussion will flourish as students assimilate and dispute information and recheck sources to come to consensus.

pare in class sends a strong message that you believe preparation is important.

As we've seen, simply telling students, "Now think about this question before tomorrow" won't work, either. They need some sort of formalized way to do that, such as journals or discussion planning sheets, which I describe in this section. Writing requires students to sift through what they know and separate relevant from irrelevant information. It also provides a rehearsal step so that information is "at

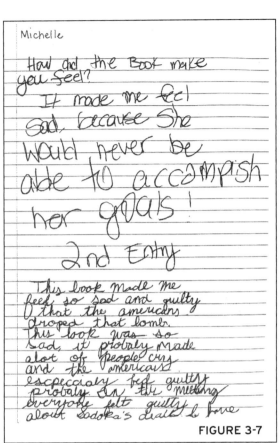

Michelle

How did the Book make you feel?

It made me feel sad, because She would never be able to accomplish her goals!

2nd Entry

This book made me feel so sad and guilty that the americans droped that bomb. This book was so sad, it probaly made alot of people cry and the americans escpecialy feel guilty probaly. In the meeting everyone felt guilty I love about Sadoka's death.

FIGURE 3-7

I feel guilty about us Americans dropping a atom bomb. If I was born back when sadako was in American, I would try to stop them from dropping the bomb. It was sad.

FIGURE 3-8

before
6/3/97 How did the book make you fell?

This book made me fell sad because she was dieing and she couldn't even fold a crane. It was good that she got to spend the last few days with her family at her house. It was also good that she never gave up she just kept up hope. I felt sad.

6/3/97 After
I still fell the same. It is just so sad because we droped the bomb. It just makes me fell bad!

FIGURE 3-9

Entry: Re, Sadako and the thousand paper crane
How did this book make you feel?
6/3 This book was pretty sad at the end. I almost cryed but I held back my tears. It was some ending. Very Emotional. I was sad because Sadako had the dream to become a great runner and it was shattered by her sickness. I thought it was nice of her friend to bring her the gold crane because it gave her hope. I also gave me hope even though I know she dies. I thought it was a great book.
After This book also made me feel bad to be an American knowing that we were the ones that dropped the bombs and the radiation killed Sadako. It was very sad.

FIGURE 3-10

the tip of the tongue" for discussion. Finally, journals and discussion planning sheets make available records of thinking to which the student can return for continued reflection and revision.

JOURNALS

Journals provide a loosely structured way for students to write their thoughts about questions and topics. Before the discussion, journals can help them gather their thoughts; after the discussion, journals promote reflection, and reflection may lead to revision of ideas. In Figure 3-7, you see how Michelle, a fifth grader, prepared for discussion of Eleanor Coerr's *Sadako and the Thousand Paper Cranes* (1977). In Figures 3-8 to 3-10, you

Classroom Discussion

see how every member of the group focuses on a new idea introduced during the discussion. All of these journal entries clearly show that an important discussion took place. (See Chapter 5 for more information on using journals for reflection.)

DISCUSSION PLANNING SHEET

A more structured form of written preparation is the Discussion Planning Sheet. (See Figure 3-11 and Appendix 6.) It gets students ready for discussion by requiring them to

◆ identify important facts they want to discuss,

◆ separate facts from opinions,

◆ come to tentative conclusions based on facts and opinions.

The Discussion Planning Sheet also provides space for students to write down thoughts that arise as a result of the discussion, reminding students that reflection is part of the discussion process.

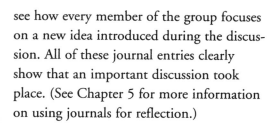

FIGURE 3-11: The Discussion Planning Sheet helps students prepare for discussion and gather thoughts for post-discussion reflection.

Developing Guidelines for Discussion

Another important aspect of preparing for discussion is developing a set of guidelines. Many teachers develop guidelines with the help of the class rather than imposing their own. But regardless of the direction you take, guidelines should cover ways to act and interact responsibly to foster community and promote rich, high-quality discussion.

Presenting guidelines in the form of questions encourages students to continuously reflect on their behavior in groups. These questions should be prominently displayed in the classroom and revisited as often as necessary.

Am I Contributing to Our Classroom Community in This Discussion?

1. Did I listen to what other people had to say?

2. Did I let people finish what they wanted to say?

3. If I disagreed, did I do it nicely?

4. If people disagreed with me, did I receive their criticism politely?

5. Did I take my turn and try not to talk all the time?

6. Did I encourage everyone to contribute? Did I show them I valued their ideas?

Am I Contributing to the Quality of the Discussion?

1. Did I do the reading or other assignment?

2. Did I prepare for the discussion by writing down my ideas?

3. Did I speak up and share my ideas?

4. Did I give facts or examples to back up my opinions?

5. Did I ask others to tell more about their ideas or to clarify their ideas?

6. Was I open-minded and willing to change my ideas and learn from the discussion?

My colleagues and I (Day et al., 2002) found an enjoyable way to engage fifth graders in thinking about guidelines for discussion. We wrote a script of a literature discussion in which each of us exhibited a different kind of inappropriate behavior. For example, Janet McLellan modeled being a "space cadet," acting inattentive and absentminded. We then staged and videotaped our discussion in front of the class. The students loved watching us behave badly, and quickly developed a set of rules to prevent that kind of behavior in discussions.

Final Thought

Preparing your class for discussion is challenging work! There are so many factors to take into account: the climate of the classroom, the size and composition of the groups, the nature of the questions asked, and guidelines for appropriate behavior and staying on task. But without careful preparation, you are likely to be disappointed in the quality of discussion in your classroom. So take the time to prepare, as challenging as it may be. You and your students will enjoy the results.

In the next chapter, we look at making discussion go smoothly. Even when students are well prepared, discussion can falter. Keeping it moving and engaging all members of the group require specific measures. In Chapter 4, I show you how to facilitate discussions to make them as productive as possible.

Classroom Discussion

Chapter Four

Facilitating Discussion: Scaffolding Instruction to Help Students Take Off

Discussion needs to be facilitated by you, your students, or all of you together; otherwise it runs the risk of stalling, losing focus, or becoming perfunctory or even mean-spirited. Consensus from those who study discussion is fairly clear: Teachers are important facilitators of whole-class discussion, but students may actually have better discussions in small groups without a teacher's presence (Almasi, 1995). Evidence shows that students can facilitate effective discussions once they have received guidance in developing the necessary strategies, such as how to invite participation and keep the group focused (Alvermann et al., 1996). This is especially true for

students in the intermediate and middle grades, but students in earlier grades can also successfully run small-group discussions. In this chapter, I describe teaching strategies for scaffolding students during discussions—carefully guiding them toward new understandings and skills. Then I show you how students can implement these strategies themselves for success.

In Chapter 3, we saw that one of the most critical purposes of whole-group discussion is to prepare students for small-group work through scaffolding. The teacher identifies a problem, gives an example, suggests a strategy, models the strategy, and gives the students opportunities to practice the strategy. Let's see how all those things happen in the following example:

TEACHER *[identifies the problem]*: When I visit your discussion groups, I've noticed that often you don't react to each other's comments. Someone will make a comment and the next speaker will say something completely unrelated, as if the first person didn't say anything. Here's a pretend example: Mary Ann said, "I think Cinderella should have run away." And right after that Jack said, "Cinderella's stepmother was really mean." You can't have a good discussion if you don't respond to each other's ideas. Jack might have asked "Why? What good would it have done Cinderella to run away?" to get Mary Ann to say more about her idea. Or he might have said, "I agree. Her life was miserable. She wouldn't have been any more miserable homeless." That takes Mary Ann's idea and adds to it. Or Jack might have disagreed: "No, she should have stayed and fought. She could have gone on strike." Those three strategies—asking for more, agreeing, or disagreeing—help keep a discussion going. *[suggests strategies.]* So today in our class discussion I want you to pay attention to how well we use those strategies to keep a good discussion going.
[introduces a question for discussion; models the strategies for a few minutes, beginning with "asking for more."]

CARLOS: But if the school system redistricts, I may have to change my school.

TEACHER: Why would that be bad?

[The discussion continues with the teacher modeling all three strategies several times.]

TEACHER: We seem to be having a good discussion. Who notices what I did to keep the discussion going?

[Students point out the use of strategies.]

TEACHER: Now I am going to let you run the class discussion. Try to use these strategies. Then we'll talk about how well the strategies worked.
[gives the students opportunities to practice.]

Scaffolding is based on the work of Lev Vygotsky (1978), who emphasized the teacher's role in learning. He advocated beginning instruction by determining what students can do, then determining what they can do with assistance, and then gradually moving them to that point through modeling and practice until they are capable of doing the activity independently.

Judith Langer (1992) identified four factors necessary for effective discussion: tapping students' understandings, inviting participation, orchestrating the discussion, and seeking clarification. Through careful scaffolding, you can teach students to carry out these tasks independently. In the sections that follow, we look at each factor, see how to scaffold it in whole-group discussion, and learn how to help students implement it in small-group discussions.

Tap Students' Understandings: Developing Ownership of the Discussion

By "tapping students' understandings," Langer (1992) means indicating to students that discussion should be about their ideas, not yours. You don't want students to think that the point of discussion is to figure out what you want them to say. If all they do is try to please you, at best they will report ideas to show off what they know, and at worst, they will be silent because of their fear of judgment.

Guidelines for Tapping Students' Understandings

Here are some ways you can help students understand that it is important for them to discuss their own ideas.

◆ **Stand out of the way if the students are moving the discussion forward without your guidance.** But if they're not, and the dialogue begins to falter, be sure to have a goal and some questions planned to start things up. A great question is "What do you think?" A bad comment is "Here's what I think." The more you tell students what you think, the less they will value their own and their classmates' ideas.

◆ **Listen before you speak.** The less you talk about what you know, the more likely you are to learn something new.

◆ **If you ask questions, ask questions as a participant, not as a leader.** Ask questions for which you don't have the answer.

◆ **Try not to evaluate students' comments.** If you judge their responses ("Raphael is right on target there." "Sue, you're ignoring an important aspect of . . ."), students will hand you the responsibility for challenging ideas and seeking clarification and will not learn those skills themselves. Further, students' comments will dry up because the participants will offer only ideas that they think you will bless. If you want convergent thinking, tell the students when you think they are right and wrong. But if you want divergent thinking, let the students evaluate one another's responses.

HELPING STUDENTS IMPLEMENT THE TASK INDEPENDENTLY

If you have modeled tapping understandings effectively, students will use their knowledge and ideas in their small-group discussion (and hopefully whole-class discussions, too). They will show evidence that they know discussion is about their ideas—not yours—in at least three ways:

◆ **Willingness to identify a focus and stick to it.** Donna Alvermann and her colleagues (1996) found that eighth graders recognized when they were off topic and understood that it made for a less productive discussion. The fifth graders that my colleagues and I (Day et al., 2002) worked with frequently repeated the prompt (the focus question) during their discussions in an effort to keep the discussion on target. Even first graders can determine if they are off task and devise strategies for staying focused, such as taking turns asking questions (Crawford & Hoopingarner, 1993). Perhaps the ultimate indicator of student ownership of discussion is when the group rejects the teacher's suggested focus and chooses its own (Alvermann et al., 1996)!

◆ **Depth of discussion.** Most researchers who study classroom discussion indicate that the quality varies widely, from superficial to quite profound. If students own the discussion, they wrestle with an idea until they reach a conclusion about it or have exhausted the topic. Janice Almasi (1995) found fourth graders were fully capable of working through a conflict until the group agreed upon a new interpretation that took into account all viewpoints.

◆ **Ability to share their ideas and respond to others' ideas.** If students understand that discussion should be about their ideas, they make an effort to gather information and reflect before meeting, perhaps using response journals or "quick writes." Again, even first graders can do this (Crawford & Hoopingarner, 1993). Simple reporting, however, as described in Chapter 1, may show ownership of one's ideas but not the commitment to an exchange of ideas.

Invite Participation: Ensuring All Students Have a Voice

Discussion leaders, whether they are teachers or students, show whose opinions they value by inviting only certain people to participate and listening and responding with varying degrees of respect. If the leader rarely asks for a particular participant to share ideas or rarely finds those ideas interesting or important when they are shared, that participant is marginalized.

At the initial stages of teaching students how to discuss, you need to invite participation by indicating who is to talk and soliciting responses. Both invitations must be part of a conscious plan: you need to be aware of who is talking too little or too much, and call on students accordingly.

Guidelines for Inviting Participation

◆ Model how to involve everyone in whole-class discussion. Keep track of who talks, using an unobtrusive checklist, and make a point of inviting into the discussion students who have not yet been heard. You may even point out students who have been heard a bit too much and make it clear that it's time for someone else to talk: "Barbara has shared several ideas. How about someone else now?"

- Be sure that you and student discussion leaders don't just invite the most knowledgeable or academically successful students to participate. A classroom discussion should reflect the entire spectrum of ideas held by the class, not just those of the most vocal or advanced. Some of the best ideas may come from a student whose thinking is not constrained by a wealth of prior knowledge on the subject.

- Expand on the comments of students, and encourage them (especially those who are quiet or unsure) to expand on their own ideas: "Tell me more." "That reminds me of . . ." "Another example of that is . . . ." Nothing discourages participation more than a comment that sits unnoticed.

- Keep track of who says what so you can attribute ideas to speakers and let them know that their ideas have been heard. Say things such as "As Margaret just said . . ." and "I want to go back to the point Kenny made."

- If you suspect a student is not participating because of lack of confidence, gently warn the student that you will be asking for an opinion soon. Say, for instance, "John, we haven't had a chance to hear from you yet. Carmen is going to tell us her ideas now, but we'd like to hear from you when Carmen is done." This gives the student an opportunity to prepare.

- Step in if a student is dominating the discussion and the others don't know how to put a stop to it. Model how to do it gently with comments such as "Wow! Ling Yu just gave us three ideas in a row. Time to hear from someone else" or "Greta, you've been doing a lot of the talking. The others need a turn. Jot down your ideas and, when we've heard from the rest of the group, we can get back to you."

- Teach students to control their body language when a participant makes an unexpected, bizarre, or just plain incorrect comment. Make it clear that rolling their eyes at a remark, heaving a loud, exasperated sigh, or folding their arms and leaning back with a bored expression can be hurtful and can stifle discussion. So it is their responsibility to avoid such insensitive behavior. Have some frank discussion about this in class, with students modeling body language that has interfered with past discussions. Then ask them to keep an eye on themselves.

A SAMPLE WHOLE-CLASS DISCUSSION IN WHICH THE TEACHER INVITES PARTICIPATION

TEACHER: Today we are going to discuss a problem we are having: leaving our tables in the lunchroom a mess when we are done eating. Has anyone noticed that problem?

GEORGEANNE: Our table is already a mess when we get there. The fifth graders eat before us and they don't clean up.

PETER: Yeah, but we don't help. We just add to the mess.

GEORGEANNE: But it isn't our fault! Why should we clean up if they don't?

ROSARIO: Because we can't control what they do, but we can control what we do.

GEORGEANNE: That's not fair.

TEACHER *[keeping track of who talks and what they say; seeking involvement of others]*: Georgeanne feels strongly about this issue, but Peter and Rosario have a different opinion. Micah, we haven't heard from you. What do you think?

MICAH: We need to clean up our own mess.

TEACHER: So you agree with Rosario and Peter?

MICAH: Yes.

GEORGEANNE: But—

TEACHER *[stepping in and encouraging expansion]*: Georgeanne, we want to hear more of what Micah has to say. Micah, why do you think we need to clean up our own mess?

MICAH: Because that's what you're supposed to do.

HELPING STUDENTS IMPLEMENT THE TASK INDEPENDENTLY

Hopefully, through your scaffolding, you have made students aware of the importance of having all group members participate. Using Talk Tokens, identifying a Tally Master, and choosing a Discussion Leader are three strategies students can use to be sure that all voices are heard in discussions.

◆ **Talk Tokens.** A Talk Token is an object such as a poker chip that stands for an opportunity to talk during the discussion. All students receive the same number of Talk Tokens at the beginning of the discussion. As students make contributions to the discussion, they place one token in the middle of the table. When students run out of tokens, their "talk time" is up and they can only make additional contributions after the others in the group have used up their tokens or have indicated they have nothing else to contribute. Talk Tokens encourage participation in two ways: They restrict dominant students from monopolizing the discussion, and they encourage reticent students to share more of their ideas.

◆ **Tally Master.** The Tally Master keeps track of how many contributions each student makes. (See Figure 4-1.) As with Talk Tokens, a Tally Master helps the group identify the students who contribute many (perhaps too many) comments to the dis-

Tally Master Record	
Name	**Turns**
Jeff	✓ ✓
Susie	✓ ✓ ✓
Devon	
Lars	✓ ✓✓ ✓ ✓
me (Lamont)	✓ ✓

FIGURE 4-1: The Tally Master's job is to keep track of who contributes to the discussion.

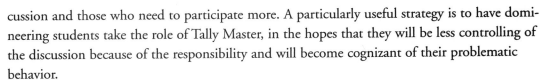

cussion and those who need to participate more. A particularly useful strategy is to have domineering students take the role of Tally Master, in the hopes that they will be less controlling of the discussion because of the responsibility and will become cognizant of their problematic behavior.

◆ **Discussion Leader.** The Discussion Leader's job is to encourage the active participation of all group members. Saying things such as, "Jeremy, we haven't heard from you in a while. What do you think?" or "We know what Cameron and LaChonya think about this, but we don't know what George and Russell think." The role of Discussion Leader should rotate through the entire group so that all students have the opportunity to take charge.

Orchestrate the Discussion: Gaining and Maintaining Momentum

If a well-orchestrated discussion were made into a fabric pattern, it would look less like pinstripes and more like paisley: not linear, but recursive, with false starts, repetitions, connections, agreements, disagreements, and modifications. If we model how to connect ideas during a discussion, how to respond to one another's ideas by extending the thought, and how to agree and disagree respectfully, students will learn to lead their own discussions.

Neil Mercer (1995) has identified three kinds of talk that might occur in a discussion. Only one kind, exploratory, advances discussion, so it needs to be encouraged, and the other kinds of talk need to be discouraged.

◆ **Disputational talk** revolves around disagreements, so it does not help the group move toward a discussion goal. It is often short but never sweet, and goes nowhere.

> **MARVIN:** Mozart was a great composer.
>
> **TAYLOR:** Beethoven was better.
>
> **MARVIN:** Oh, Mozart was much better than Beethoven.
>
> **TAYLOR:** You don't know anything.

◆ **Cumulative talk** is additive (idea + idea + idea) but uncritical, so it really doesn't move discussion forward. Xue makes a comment, Arthur expands upon it, Annie essentially repeats what Xue said, and Melvin confirms Annie's comments. Four contributions advance the discussion by just one step, because all the ideas are basically the same. An even less fruitful form of cumulative talk is reporting, in which one participant makes a comment, the next participant adds an unrelated comment, and a third contributes yet another.

- **Procedural talk** was not mentioned by Mercer, but my colleagues and I (Day et al., 2002) found that it tended to dominate many discussions. Students often get bogged down talking about what should be happening rather than about ideas: who should talk next, what the prompt is or should be for the next discussion, how many pages should be read before the next meeting, and so on.
- **Exploratory talk** is the most productive kind of talk, according to Mercer. Participants counter one another's contributions, ask for evidence and reasons, and suggest alternate hypotheses. (The guidelines that follow show you how to orchestrate exploratory talk.)

Talented leaders orchestrate discussion unconsciously. They seem to have an instinct for encouraging exploratory talk, for knowing when to clarify an idea and when to leave it for others to clarify, when to help out and when to let a participant struggle a bit, when to continue discussing a point and when to shift gears. For the rest of us, some guidelines can help.

Guidelines for Orchestrating the Discussion

- Model how to orchestrate discussion for the whole class. Be aware of the strategies you use and name them to help students remember them. For example, "Is This What You Mean?" could identify a strategy that shows how repeating your understanding of someone's ideas invites the speaker to clarify and extend those ideas. "Been There, Done That" could identify a strategy for moving the discussion along when ideas get too repetitive.

DISCUSSION STIFLER

"Coming to the Rescue"

"Rescuing" someone in a discussion by supplying a word or idea that the person is struggling to bring to mind or by clarifying a concept the person is having difficulty expressing doesn't help. It just prevents the rescued person from benefiting from the discussion. I used to be the Queen of Rescuers, thinking I was being attentive and participatory, showing I was interested in what other people had to say and following their arguments. But as a psychiatrist friend pointed out, when you rescue someone, you are actually saying, "I think you are too dumb to find that word or express that idea without help" and "I don't have time to wait for you to come up with the word or idea." It's a fine line between being a Facilitator and being a Rescuer!

- Wait, be quiet, and let students lead and orchestrate when they can. Once you have modeled a strategy, give students the opportunity to use it.
- But after you have waited, don't be afraid to point out inconsistencies and provide correct information. As the teacher, you have a responsibility to ensure the students' understanding of the curriculum, not just discussion techniques. And discussion based on incorrect information or faulty logic is not a good discussion!
- Occasionally use Think Alouds with your modeling. When you think aloud, you share your thinking behind a strategy by talking about your process as you model the strategy. Here are excerpts from a whole-class discussion about the Founding Fathers and the Constitution, in which the teacher thinks aloud to demonstrate the strategy of "Tell Me More," which encourages clarification:

    JAMAAL: I think those old guys were sexist.

    TEACHER: I want to know more about what Jamaal is saying. Watch how I do this. "Jamaal, your point that the Founding Fathers seemed sexist is interesting. Tell us why you think that. Share your evidence with us." See how I let him know that his idea was valuable, so he didn't feel threatened, but that he hadn't told us enough yet.

    [The class continues the discussion. The comments about sexism have become repetitive and new ideas have not been offered for a while.]

    TEACHER: You've made several interesting points about the possible sexism of the men who wrote the Constitution. Now let's move on to talking about why the Bill of Rights was needed. But before we do that, tell me what did I just do to shift the discussion to another topic?

    You can use Think Alouds "forward," by telling the students what you are about to do (as with Jamaal), or "backward," by asking students to tell you what you just did. If the students can't identify the strategy, tell them what you did. However, don't overuse Think Alouds—they can be disruptive. One or two a discussion is plenty.
- Watch students' body language for boredom, confusion, and restlessness and show how to use these as signals to move the discussion forward more briskly, to slow down for clarification, and so on.

HELPING STUDENTS IMPLEMENT THE TASK INDEPENDENTLY

Connect and Extend are basic strategies for orchestrating a discussion.

- **Connect** keeps the discussion moving by reiterating an idea just stated so listeners know why the next idea makes sense.
- **Extend** keeps the discussion moving by adding new information. This can be done by asking a speaker to provide more information, by agreeing with a comment and adding to it, or by disagreeing and telling why. Let's see how this works.

[The students are discussing how to design an experiment to measure the speed of sound in air.]

EMILIO: We need something to make a big sound, a really loud one.

KARLOTTA: *[Connect]* Right, Emilio, it has to be loud *[Extend—adding new information]* because we need to be far away to measure the speed.

JANICE: *[Extend—asking for more information]* Why do we have to be far away?

KARLOTTA: Because sound travels really fast. If we are close to the sound, we won't be able to meas-ure it, because we'll see someone making the sound at the same time we hear it. We have to be far away so we can see the person making the sound but the sound doesn't get to us right away.

EMILIO: *[Connect]* First, let's figure out how to make the sound. It has to be loud and we have to be able to see someone making it.

JANICE: *[Extend]* How about banging on a pipe with a hammer? *[Connect]* That's loud and you could see someone doing it.

Model Connect and Extend for your class and post a chart like the one shown in Figure 4-2 to remind students to use these strategies in their small-group discussions.

> ## Connect and Extend
>
> **Connect your comment with what someone else has said.**
> - ◆ "Bob just said . . ."
> - ◆ "Claire's point that . . ."
>
> **Extend the idea by asking for more information. . .**
> - ◆ "Tell me more about . . ."
> - ◆ "Give me another example of . . ."
>
> **. . . or by adding your own information:**
> - ◆ "I agree because . . ."
> - ◆ "I disagree because . . ."
>
> FIGURE 4-2

Seek Clarification: Building Understanding

Discussion prospers when participants present their ideas clearly and are so committed to the success of the discussion that they ask probing questions to better understand ideas. Discussion falters when partic-ipants are interested only in their own points of view and don't care if they understand what others are saying. In other words, in true discussion participants seek clarification to ensure they understand.

Guidelines for Seeking Clarification

◆ Prepare the students to request clarification. All teachers have had the frustrating and sometimes hilarious experience of asking students for clarification and receiving a completely unexpected response. For example, I've heard 25 sweet little voices chirp "Happy" when I've asked how a character felt. And when I asked, "Are you sure?" the same 25 sweet little voices immediately, without missing a beat, chirped "Sad." Aargh! This happens, I believe, because students are used to being asked for clarification or proof only when they are wrong. So prepare them by telling them that, in discussions, you and others will be asking them questions such as, "Are you sure?" "What proof do you have?" and "Can you say that another way so that I understand it better?" Warn them that you are going to ask these questions whether you agree or disagree with what they have said. If your students are particularly threatened by such questions, as an interim measure you might first validate their response: "Trudy, that is a great answer, but I need to know more." "I think I agree with your idea, Bill, but can you tell me how you arrived at that conclusion?"

◆ With the class, develop a list of questions that students can use to ask for clarification without being confrontational, including questions that express disagreement civilly. Post the list and encourage students to refer to it as needed. (See Figure 4-3 for a possible list.)

◆ Move students forward in their thinking through Focusing and Shaping—two aspects of scaffolding (Langer, 1992) that help them clarify their own ideas. When students understand strategies for making their own ideas clear, they more easily see ways to seek clarification in discussion.

FOCUSING

Students often need help focusing on a specific idea, clarifying for themselves the exact point they wish to make. Without a clear focus, their idea may be so broad that it is misunderstood or subsumed by another idea. To help students focus, you might ask, "Now tell me just one thing you want us to remember about what you have just said," "That sounds a lot like what Abe said. How is your idea different from Abe's?" or "Here are three points you just made. *[List them on the board.]* What do those three points add up to?"

SHAPING

Students also often need help in presenting ideas succinctly. If a participant rambles on and introduces extraneous information, listeners will not only be unable to discern the main idea, but they won't care and certainly won't ask the speaker to

---

What to Say When You Don't Understand

Repeat what the person said.

◆ "You said that . . . What do you mean by that? Can you say it in a different way?"

Disagree politely.

◆ "I don't agree. Here's why . . ."
◆ "That's not how I was thinking about it."
◆ "Here's another way to think about that."

Ask where an idea comes from.

◆ "I don't understand how you came to that conclusion. Can you tell me your reasoning?"
◆ "I may be missing something here. What made you think that?"

FIGURE 4-3

Semantic Webbing: Determining if Clarification Is Needed

In Chapter 2, I described how to use Semantic Webbing to help students organize facts into higher-level concepts by categorizing their responses. For example, students might give ideas on how to discourage smoking and categorize their responses as "governmental actions" or "personal actions," or categorize the characteristics of Baroque paintings as "content," "composition," or "form." Semantic Webbing is an excellent way to determine if clarification is needed in discussion because responses cannot be categorized appropriately if not understood. Here's how it works:

1. As the students discuss a question, jot their responses in no particular order on the chalkboard. (See Figure 2-8 on page 49.)

2. After all responses have been shared, ask students to web (categorize) them by putting together ideas that seem to go together. To determine if the ideas are clear, do not allow students to web their own responses. For example, in a discussion of stealing, if Meiko introduced the idea that downloading music from the Internet is theft, do not permit her to categorize this idea on the web. Another participant should restate the idea and categorize it to ensure that Meiko's response makes sense to others.

3. Responses that are not webbed are probably not understood and, therefore, need to be clarified. For example, if no one offers to categorize "plagiarism" in the discussion of stealing, then it is likely the students do not understand that concept and how it relates to theft. Ask the participant who offered the response to clarify it. Responses that are paraphrased incorrectly or categorized inappropriately will also need clarification.

say more for purposes of clarification! (The mini-lesson on shaping an idea on page 98 may help.) The "quick write" is a shaping strategy in which students are given a few minutes to jot down their ideas before the discussion, so that they can organize their thoughts rather than just speak extemporaneously.

HELPING STUDENTS IMPLEMENT THE TASK INDEPENDENTLY

Students who are committed to understanding ask for and provide clarification during discussion. In the following example, note the lack of commitment, as illustrated by three related but vague ideas about Victorian England.

Example of a Discussion in Which Students Do Not Seek Clarification

TEACHER: Can you describe Victorian England, based on how Dickens portrays it in *Oliver Twist*?

BRUCE: It was nasty.

LEAH: It wasn't a good place to be if you were poor.

DOMINICK: I wouldn't have wanted to live there.

Contrast this with the example below, in which students challenge the same unclear ideas and ask for clarification.

Example of a Discussion in Which Students Seek Clarification

BRUCE: It was nasty.

DIANE: What do you mean by "nasty"?

MINI-LESSON

Shaping an Idea

Objectives: To help students understand that an idea must be presented succinctly, without distracting, extraneous information; to help students understand the importance of staging information so that one idea leads to another and that, together, the ideas add up to one big idea.

Materials: Markers; two or three examples of paragraphs with a lot of distracting, extraneous information, such as:

> Bullies are dumb and mean. Really big kids pick on little kids. Teachers need to do something about bullies. Bullies are scary. I don't like bullies. We have too many bullies in our school. We have cheaters in our school too. These kids cheat on tests and copy each other's homework. And another thing that bothers me is that kids butt in line in the lunchroom. That's not fair.

Reproduce the paragraph on an overhead transparency, chart paper, or the board.

Steps:

1. Display one of the paragraphs. Be sure all students can see it.

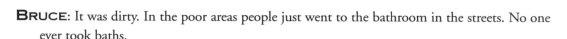

BRUCE: It was dirty. In the poor areas people just went to the bathroom in the streets. No one ever took baths.

DIANE: Yeah. It was also nasty because people got sick more and died easier than now.

LEAH: It wasn't a good place to be if you were poor.

BRUCE: Why was it so much worse if you were poor?

LEAH: If you were rich, you had servants to clean up after you. And if you were rich you had food and a house. But if you were poor, no one cared. And you got thrown in awful jails for nothing if you were poor.

DOMINICK: I wouldn't have wanted to live there.

LEAH: Why? I wouldn't have minded it if I had been rich, all those servants and pretty clothes. And I love horses, so it would have been neat to have had horses for my carriages.

2. Read it and ask the class to identify the problems. Students may suggest (1) there are too many different ideas, (2) some of the information is off topic, and (3) there are no examples, evidence, or proof.

3. Have students suggest ways to eliminate these problems, such as (1) crossing out the extraneous information (such as the passage about cheaters), (2) isolating the remaining "big ideas" and writing one focused sentence about each, (3) providing one or two specific examples or extensions for each big idea.

4. Show the students a contribution to a discussion that is too succinct, such as "Bullies are just awful." Ask them to clarify this idea by providing one or two examples. Then ask them to return to the model sentence and find a more precise description than "just awful."

5. Repeat the procedure using one or two other sample paragraphs.

6. Lead students to the understanding that a discussion may make several points, and each well-presented discussion point has these characteristics:

   a. It makes just one point.

   b. It makes the point early and in one sentence.

   c. One or two examples can be used to extend or clarify the point, but more than that can be distracting.

DOMINICK: Yeah, but even the rich got sick and died, and they didn't have television or computers.

As a result of their requests for clarification, students begin to develop a picture of Victorian England. In the first example this does not happen because students are not committed to the task and, therefore, end up with comments that could describe any place and time.

Final Thought

Facilitating discussion means preparing students carefully and then letting go of the reins. It does not mean serving as the Discussion Leader yourself. If you do a thorough job of scaffolding—tapping student understandings, inviting participation, orchestrating discussions, and modeling how to seek clarification—your students will be able to lead their own discussions, with you in the role of either participant or observer.

In the next chapter, we explore how follow-up work provides the opportunity for students to continue to revise and refine their ideas.

Chapter Five

Following Up Discussion: Keeping the Thinking Alive

I f a discussion has been effective, participants leave with new perspectives and meanings. But this should not be the end of meaning-making. After discussion, students should continue to reflect, consolidate, and refine their new perspectives and meanings. This rarely happens spontaneously; most students need to be given time and direction.

Our experience with students as writers, for example, teaches us that they do not view revision as a natural step in the writing process. Students are often surprised at the suggestion that they revise their writing. They view the task as producing a piece of writing, not producing a piece of high-quality writing. Similarly, many students view participation as the goal of discussion, not gaining perspectives and making meaning. So the idea that these processes might continue once discussion has ended seems strange.

Mini-lessons, reflection journals, and thinking charts ensure that students continue gaining perspectives and making meaning long after the discussion is over. In this chapter, I discuss these approaches in depth.

Mini-Lessons

Through whole-class mini-lessons like the one below, you can help students realize the importance of continuing thinking after discussion has ended.

MINI-LESSON

Continuing Thinking After Discussion

Objectives: To help students recognize that their ideas change as a result of interacting with others and learning the ideas of others.

Materials: Paper and pencils, chart paper, markers, photocopies of the Continuing Thinking After Discussion chart (Appendix 7).

Steps:

1. Engage students in a discussion of how their ideas have changed through discussion. Be prepared to give one or two examples of how, in the past, you have changed your idea about a topic after discussing it with another person. For example, you might have felt it appropriate to give an hour's homework to your class Monday through Thursday. Then you learned that several other teachers all had that plan, which made for five hours of home- work every night. So you worked out a schedule with your colleagues so that on Mondays students did science homework, on Tuesday language arts, and so on. As you give your examples, fill in the Continuing Thinking After Discussion chart on the board or chart paper. (See Figure 5-1.) Then fill in another chart using examples from students.

---

2. Emphasize that we grow as learners when we gain new perspectives, get new information, and listen to others. And we don't grow if we refuse to rethink our ideas. But be sure the class understands that while discussion doesn't always lead to a change of mind, the potential must always be there.

3. Distribute photocopies of the Continuing Thinking After Discussion chart and introduce a topic that will invite varying opinions, such as "How would you change the length of terms in Congress? Give your rationale," or "Design the ideal cafeteria menu for combating obesity." Give the students three to five minutes to fill in the first column, "What I Originally Thought."

Continuing Thinking After Discussion

What I Originally Thought	New Information From Others	What I Think Now
Ms. Miller—give 1 hr. homework M–Th	all the other teachers were also going to do that	We agreed science homework would be Mon, math on Tues, S.S. on Wed, & lang art on Thurs.
Raoul —thought his dad should buy a BMW	found out the price!	Is happy with a new Toyota
Sarah — smoking doesn't cause cancer	read an article, with pictures	smoking can cause cancer

FIGURE 5-1

4. Divide the class into discussion groups. Try to ensure that differing perspectives are represented in each group. (See the discussion of U-Debates on page 67 for inspiration.) Give groups 10 to 15 minutes to discuss the topic.

5. At the end of the allotted time, have students complete the second column, "New Information From Others." If students feel that they have nothing to write in that column, other group members should help out.

6. Let the ideas simmer. After at least 24 hours have passed, bring the class together and ask each student to fill in the third column, "What I Think Now." Have a class discussion about what *change* means (complete reversal, slight modification, expanded concept, and so on), why ideas changed, and why ideas didn't change.

Reflection Journals

Journals can also assist students in gaining perspectives and making meaning, especially if students make entries before and after discussion.

> Mitten Madness Prompt: Have you ever felt like the caracter in the story?
>
> B
> Yes + No Yes because a have a brother that is like her. No because I don't have a sister
>
> A
> Now I feel like Carla because I have a pillow that I like, and I always sleep on it everytime I have a brother that is a noreine.

FIGURE 5-2

The students in Jeni Day's fifth-grade class prepared for literature circles by writing their thoughts about their readings in their journals. After each meeting, the students made a second entry. Sometimes students wrote about how their thinking changed as a result of discussion.

> 2/10 The Midwifes Apprentice
> No, I Never felt like eanybody in this book but if I did I will probaley run away.
>
> I changed my mind yes I felt like the girl in the book. One time I was trying to make cookeis for my Jmom's birthday and they burnt so I threw them in the trash.

FIGURE 5-3

> Before- I think he did, If he didn't Alma would be dead. If I cared about someone like he did I would do the same. I think Jackson is very brave and had alot of confidence in getting to Avondale.
>
> people thought that Jackson have drove the car or tried Alma but he cares for I kept the same deccion.

FIGURE 5-4

> 2/11   Cracker Jackson
> Before: No I would not do what the main character did he was risking his life.
> AFTER: I still don't think that I would have done what Cracker Jackson did because he could died.

FIGURE 5-5

Occasionally students explicitly stated that their thinking had not changed.

```
1 entry
Yes because It's a smart trick and I
want to learn more like that


2 entry

   I think there was a point to the
story "Not to be greedy" but angel alex
and Daniel are saying that there was
no point to the story
```

FIGURE 5-6

Students took notice of others' ideas. Sometimes they reported group consensus.

```
Entry #1    Have you ever felt like
            a character in the story?

       Yes, I have felt like the birds before.
Someone asked me to do something and
I put it off 'til later. I've also felt
like the bat. Making a promise and
breaking it and feeling real bad. Also
feeling like I have to do something
by myself and feeling like can't and
won't be able to do it.
After   My group didn't have much to say
BC   about feeling like other characters.
But one thing Ashley said caught
my attention. She said that she had
felt like the bat by having such a
big responsibility and now that I
think about it the bat had a lot
on her hands and if I had that
much to do I'd be stressed out too.
```

FIGURE 5-7

```
   2nd entry
   I think that my favorite
part was when either
he made a home run,
or when the guy in
the tower gave him
a thumbs up sign. The
man-in-the-tower part
seemed to be a majority
in our group.
```

FIGURE 5-8

Page 82 shows particularly poignant journal reflections by girls who discussed Eleanor Coerr's *Sadako and the Thousand Paper Cranes* (1977).

MINI-LESSON

Reflecting on Reflection Journals

Objective: To make students aware of the degree to which their ideas are or are not changing as a result of discussion.

Materials: Copies of at least four pairs of pre- and postdiscussion student journal entries: at least two showing change and two showing no change (see Figures 5-2 through 5-8 for examples); copies of Analyzing Reflection Journal Entries chart (Appendix 8) for each student.

Steps:

1. After students have made several pairs of pre- and postdiscussion entries, bring them together to remind them that the purposes of keeping journals are to encourage reflection and continued thinking and to record how ideas change as a result of discussion and continued thinking. Tell them that today they are going to examine their journals to see how much their thinking changed.

2. Show the class the two examples of paired entries that demonstrate change. One example should show a fairly dramatic shift in opinion, an "aha!" moment, such as the ones in Figures 5-2 and 5-3. The other example should be more subtle, showing an elaboration or slight shift in opinion. Label the first example "Aha!" and the second example "Yes, I Can See That." By seeing both kinds of examples, students understand that change has many forms.

3. Show the class the third example, such as Figures 5-6 through 5-8, in which the writer has maintained the original opinion but shown awareness that different perspec-

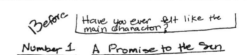

Before | Have you ever felt like the main character?

Number 1   A Promise to the Sun

I have felt like the main Carikter because some times I maked promise and I don't keep it. I liked the part with the sun helped the earth but I did not like the story.

Number 2   After

I think that I felt like the cartter when I tell lies and I think that when I make promise to my mom and dad and don't keep them I fell like the curikter.

FIGURE 5-9

tives exist. Explain that change is not necessary if, upon reflection, the student does not think it's warranted. Label this example "Hmm, but No, Thanks."

4. Show the fourth example, the "bad" example, such as Figures 5-9 and 5-10, in which the second entry is essentially a "ditto" of the first, showing that the writer did not reflect upon the ideas of others. Label this one "No Reflection."

5. Ask students to review their own paired journal entries, labeling each

second entry as "Aha!," "Yes, I Can See That," "Hmm, but No, Thanks," or "No Reflection." Have students use the Analyzing Reflection Journal Entries chart to plot their entries on a bar graph and discuss their graphs as a class. Students who have a profile with many "No Reflections" may need further guidance in considering the voices of others. Those with all "Ahas!" may not be doing enough prediscussion thinking or may need some confidence-building activities. (See Figure 5-11 and Appendix 8.)

2/11   Cracker Jackson

Before: No I would not do what the main character did he was risking his life.

AFTER: I still don't think that I would have done what Cracker Jackson did because he could be died.

2/18   Cracker Jackson

Before: I think that Cracker did the wrong thing because he was risking his life when they could have called the police or Alma could have just left Billy Ray.

A taste of Blackberries

Prompt: Write 10 questions to ask the author

2/25

Prompt: Do you like this book better than Cracker Jackson

Answer: No I don't like this book better than C.J it is not as exciting as C.J.

After: I fell the same

FIGURE 5-10

Analyzing Reflection Journal Entries

Date	Aha!	Yes, I Can See	Hm, but No, Thanks	No Reflection
1/3	✓	✓		
2/10				✓
2/12	✓			
2/13		✓	✓	
2/17				✓
2/18			✓	
2/21		✓		

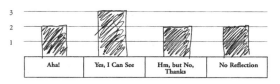

| | Aha! | Yes, I Can See | Hm, but No, Thanks | No Reflection |

FIGURE 5-11

Thinking Charts

I've found that students who are visually oriented enjoy charting their thinking, and there are tools to help them do that, including the Continuing Thinking After Discussion chart described earlier in this chapter. Other tools include K-W-L and the Discussion Planning Sheet described in Chapter 3, and Discussion Webs and the Confidence Rating Form described in Chapter 2. The Tracking My Thinking chart shown in Figure 5-12 and Appendix 9 requires students to delve more deeply into how their thinking evolved because it asks them to identify the big idea and the supporting ideas.

Tracking My Thinking

My Original Ideas	What Others Thought	What I Think Now
Big Idea There are 3 forms of energy **Support** chemical **Support** electricity nucler	Bill – sound = energy bec. of vibrations Ernesto – heat = energy	There are at least 5 forms. What about Solar? Is that heat??

FIGURE 5-12: The Tracking My Thinking chart helps students see the development of their ideas by requiring them to write down their original ideas with supporting evidence, the ideas of others raised in discussion, and their expanded ideas based on discussion.

Final Thought

As we've seen, discussion is a wonderful way to ignite intellectual fires. To keep those fires burning after discussion, your students need the classroom time and structures to reflect, both in writing and in ongoing discussion.

In the next and final chapter, we look at assessing discussion. Specifically, I show you how to gauge the various dimensions of discussion, including the quality of a discussion and what students have learned from it.

Chapter Six

Assessing Discussion: Determining if Your Efforts Are Paying Off

F or five chapters, I have encouraged you to make time in the curriculum for discussion and to use that time wisely. I have described what discussion is and is not, and I have assured you that developing expertise in preparing for and facilitating discussion takes time. This chapter is designed to help you decide if all this effort is worthwhile. This chapter is about assessment.

With increasing emphasis on accountability, we must be able to justify time spent in discussion. Parents, administrators, and even students may suggest that lecture is the best way to prepare for fact-based, standardized tests. Time given to discussion may be seen as time taken away from gaining information needed to pass those tests. Those who challenge the use of discussion may not understand or may have lost sight of parts of the curriculum that those tests don't cover, such as the development of student thinking. Further, they may not understand the potential of discussion for advancing learning—that it need not take away from the curriculum but can enhance it. Saying that, however, doesn't make it so. Discussion has the potential to enhance learning. Assessment lets you and the critics know if that potential is being reached.

The chapter begins with a framework for assessing discussion that is designed to make assessment consistent and fair. Next, I suggest general guidelines for assessing discussion within that framework. The bulk of the chapter deals with four specific, very important aspects of assessing discussion: determining if you have a discussion curriculum in place and if you've set the stage for successful classroom discussion, and assessing the quality of discussion in your classroom and what the students have learned through discussion. The chapter ends with a note on record keeping.

Develop an Overall Plan for Assessment

Assessment must be systematic. Without a plan, it is likely to be haphazard, with some strategies assessed and others not. The next sections suggest a framework for addressing four critical questions: What will be assessed? Who will carry out the assessment? How will the assessment be performed? What will be done with the results?

What Will Be Assessed?

Here are the most important aspects of classroom discussion that should be assessed. (Later in the chapter, I explain in detail how to assess each of these aspects.)

1. **Determining if You Have a Discussion Curriculum in Place**
2. **Determining if You Have Set the Stage for Successful Classroom Discussion Time**
   - Time to develop discussion strategies
   - Time to practice discussion strategies

Climate
- Development of a spirit of inquiry
- Development of trust and mutual respect

3. **Determining the Quality of Discussion in Your Classroom**
   - Preparation
   - Focus, purpose, and engagement
   - Interaction
   - Level of thinking

4. **Determining What Students Learned Through Discussion**
   - New meaning
   - Accuracy of meaning

Who Will Carry Out the Assessment?

Certainly you need to develop and carry out the assessment plan, but each group and each group member should also be involved so that the students take ownership of their own program and that of their group. Many of the procedures discussed in the next section can be carried out by either you or your students.

How Will the Assessment Be Performed?

There are many ways to gather data about the success of discussion groups. Observation records and checklists, journals, questionnaires, charts, and audio- or videotapes all can provide important information. Using more than one kind of tool provides a more accurate and complete picture. Many of the assessment tools described later in the chapter can also be used by either you or your students.

RUBRICS

Rubrics are a popular assessment tool because they help you think about the criteria you use for making decisions and organize them into an easy-to-read, easy-to-apply format. I've used the rubric here (Figure

---

Rubric: Postdiscussion Journal Entries

The student's skill in writing postdiscussion reflections is:

Well Developed	Developing	Poorly Developed
Writes in journal after discussion; entry shows evidence of reflection, e.g., consideration of other points of view, extension of ideas, supported confirmation of original ideas	Writes in journal after discussion; entry lacks evidence of reflection, e.g., consideration of other points of view, extension of ideas, supported confirmation of original ideas	Does not write in journal or the entry is very short and generic, e.g., "I liked the book."

Comments:

FIGURE 6-1: This rubric is designed to assess postdiscussion journal entries.

6-1) with great success. You'll find a reproducible version in Appendix 10.

The criteria that rubrics contain must be specific. The more specific they are, in fact, the more likely you'll be able to use results to inform and differentiate instruction. A student who does not write in the journal at all, for example, needs different guidance than a student who makes the effort but produces mediocre entries. Figure 6-2 shows that Charlie, a seventh grader, needs different instruction than Marlene, a fourth grader. Charlie sees the forest but not the trees, whereas Marlene gathers small bits of information that don't really add up to much.

What Will Be Done with the Results?

There is no point in spending time and energy on assessment if you don't do something with the results. The purpose of assessment is not to gather data but to use data to improve instruction and help students achieve goals. I call this phase in the assessment process "Next Steps." This phase helps you think about questions you need to ask next in order to provide appropriate instruction.

Name Charlie   **Date** April 4

Observation Notes:

3/18 small group. "Sources of energy"; makes two important contributions to Big Ideas but can't back them up with proof

3/26 whole group; starts us off with "Nuke energy must be regulated." but had no suggestions on how

3/28 sm. grp. offered a supporting detail for Rosario's idea

4/4 whole grp, made 2 main idea contributions; when pressed, _no_ back-up ideas

Quality	Well Developed	Developing	Poorly Developed
works with Big Ideas	develops Big Ideas on own; introduces Big Ideas into discussion	understands Big Ideas when introduced by others	does not understand Big Ideas
works with Little Ideas	uses Little Ideas to develop or support Big ideas; notes important details	notes important details but does not use them to develop or support Big Ideas	does not notice or use details

FIGURE 6-2: These examples show how using a rubric, combined with observation, can help you identify specific strengths and weaknesses in each student.

Name Marlene   **Date** 2/26

Observation Notes:

1/19 small group, Terrible Things . could give order of animals' capture but missed the whole point!

1/21 small group, Pinballs; knew what happened; could practically tell events verbatim; no idea of theme

1/28 whole class, s. studies; just doesn't understand idea of "regions"; can describe a region – sand, hills, etc.

2/19 whole class, science; gave great memorized definition of ecology but can't put it all together

Quality	Well Developed	Developing	Poorly Developed
works with Big Ideas	develops Big Ideas on own; introduces Big Ideas into discussion	understands Big Ideas when introduced by others	does not understand Big Ideas
works with Little Ideas	uses Little Ideas to develop or support Big ideas; notes important details	notes important details but does not use them to develop or support Big Ideas	does not notice or use details

Guidelines for Assessing Discussion

With so much else on your plate, having yet another thing to assess may not be all that appealing. But take heart. The guidelines below are designed to put assessment of discussion into perspective and make it manageable.

Assess No More Than Two Factors at a Time and Focus on Them Until You See Improvement

You and the students need a clear focus for each assessment. If you take on too much—for example, if you try to assess participation, level of thinking, accuracy of thinking, and engagement all at once—you will end up with shoddy, poorly gathered data. You will feel rushed because there is so much to assess, and you will miss important information because you'll be looking at too much at once. Also, remember: If you try to assess too much at one time, the assessment will take more time than the discussion!

So pick one or two factors of discussion, assess them using the techniques described later in this chapter, and develop plans for improvement. Implement the plans for improvement and keep assessing those factors until you notice improvement. After all, what is the point of assessment if you aren't going to use the data to make changes?

Prioritize What You Will Assess

If you are going to assess and work on only one or two factors, then it might make sense to assess the most important factors first, those most critical to the success of discussion. Or you might decide to work on a couple of easily fixed factors. Or you might choose one "big" factor and one "small" one. The point is to assess discussion in discrete stages. The mini-lesson on the next page will help.

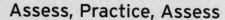

Assess, Practice, Assess

1. **Assess:** Once you or the students have identified a focus, the first assessment should identify the current level of student achievement for that skill. You will undoubtedly find a range. Belinda, Eduardo, and Lamont may be close to mastering the skill; Gina and Hans may be extremely weak; and the majority of the class will be at a point where instruction can be of benefit. This information forms a baseline and allows you to assess improvement.

2. **Practice:** The students implement their plan, practicing and trying to improve their skills.

3. **Assess:** Assessment should take place periodically (but not necessarily at each meeting). Once two or three consecutive assessments show a satisfactory level of performance, have the group select a new area of focus. If the assessment reveals no improvement, work with the group to develop a different plan for improvement, which may require you to reteach some strategies.

MINI-LESSON

Prioritizing for Assessment

Objectives: To help each discussion group identify factors important to the success of discussion; to have each group design its own assessment plan by prioritizing factors and identifying two for assessment.

Materials: Markers, chart paper.

Steps:

1. Have students meet in their discussion groups and discuss the question: What does a good discussion look like? Tell each group to appoint someone to record participants' ideas.

2. Ask the groups to report their ideas to the entire class. As ideas are presented, cluster similar ones on chart paper without labeling them. After you've created a cluster of

continued on page 116

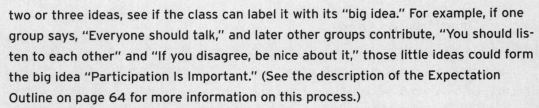

two or three ideas, see if the class can label it with its "big idea." For example, if one group says, "Everyone should talk," and later other groups contribute, "You should listen to each other" and "If you disagree, be nice about it," those little ideas could form the big idea "Participation Is Important." (See the description of the Expectation Outline on page 64 for more information on this process.)

3. Continue until all ideas have been reported from the groups, placed into clusters, and labeled with a big idea. Use the big ideas to elicit additional characteristics of a good discussion. Post the results as a chart titled "What Makes a Good Discussion."

4. Have the students return to their discussion groups. Ask each group to prioritize the big ideas numerically from "most important" to "least important." Tell students there is no right answer, but they should be able to defend their decisions.

5. Reconvene and have each group call out its prioritized list, one by one. As they do, jot their numbers next to the appropriate big ideas. Once the numbers are recorded, lead the class in a discussion of the results. If there is consensus that one idea is high in importance, ask the whole class to provide reasons. If, as is quite likely, there is little consensus, ask each group to provide its reasoning. The goal is not agreement but thoughtful consideration of each big idea.

6. The next day, ask each group to select one big idea to work on, preferably one that was high on its priority list. From there, have members prioritize the little ideas that form that big idea, select the one or two most important ones to assess, and develop plans for improvement, if needed.

Each group is apt to select a different big idea or, at the least, prioritize the little ideas differently. This is fine. In fact, it will provide material for rich class discussions about discussion in the future. Review the What Makes a Good Discussion chart periodically. Although each group has its own focus for assessment, the chart will remind them of all the factors to consider. Students should keep these factors in mind even though they haven't selected all of them for assessment. You might want to place stick-on notes next to each factor on the list to indicate which groups are currently assessing those factors. As you periodically review the chart with the whole class, have groups report their methods of assessment, plans for improvement, and success to date.

Four Important Aspects of Assessing Discussion

In this section, we explore the four important aspects of assessing discussion mentioned earlier: determining if you have a discussion curriculum in place, determining if you've set the stage for successful classroom discussion, determining the quality of discussion in your classroom, and determining what the students have learned through discussion.

Do I Have a Discussion Curriculum in Place?

Before you can assess the context, quality, and results of discussion, you must make sure that students are capable of applying the basic strategies necessary for good discussion. Here are some points to consider as you determine if you have a discussion curriculum in place. With the proper curriculum, students will be able to do the following:

Start off discussion, meaning they will
- come to discussion prepared,
- pose interesting questions and set purposes.

Participate, meaning they will
- contribute to discussion,
- listen to others,
- take turns,
- respond to others' comments,
- ask for clarification when needed,
- disagree civilly,
- be open to new ideas,
- gain new information from discussion,
- stay focused,
- sustain discussion so that some degree of depth is reached.

Think and reflect, meaning they will
- reach high levels of thinking,
- continue to reflect and revise thinking after discussion has ended.

See Appendix 11 for a reproducible version of this checklist.

Have I Set the Stage for Successful Classroom Discussion?

Setting the stage for successful classroom discussion involves two critical factors: establishing classroom time for students to develop and practice discussion strategies and establishing a climate of inquiry, trust, and mutual respect. (See Chapters 2 and 3 for more information on these factors.) The following questions will help you determine if you have built a foundation for good discussion:

Time

◆ Do the students have time to practice discussion strategies?
  • Does whole-group discussion occur daily?
  • Does small-group discussion occur at least three times each week?

Climate

◆ Have I developed a spirit of inquiry in the class?
  • Are the students comfortable with divergent ideas and lack of consensus?
  • Do the students listen to each other with open minds?
  • Do I overuse the IRE (Interrogate-Respond-Evaluate) pattern?
◆ Is there trust and mutual respect among the students?

What Is the Quality of Discussion in My Classroom?

If you truly believe that discussion is an important part of your curriculum, you need to assess the quality of your discussion. Four dimensions are important in doing that: preparation; focus, purpose, and engagement; interaction; and level of thinking. This section presents ways students can assess themselves according to these dimensions, and then it offers "next steps" to help you continue assessment.

PREPARATION

Students must come to the discussion with ideas, and you must provide access to those ideas by matching students with appropriate resources and by making certain they have critical background knowledge and vocabulary. They must complete the required assignment, whether it be reading, thinking, viewing, listening, or writing in a journal, with an eye toward gleaning information and coming to the discussion with something to say.

> See Chapter 2 for information about using response journals to prepare for discussion. See Chapter 3 for information about the teacher's role in establishing background knowledge and critical vocabulary.

Assessing Preparation

It is in the group's best interest to determine what it means to be "prepared" and to work together to assess how well each participant meets those criteria. This can be done in a very straightforward manner:

1. The group identifies the criteria for being prepared. They may decide, for example, that before discussion each member should (*a*) do the assigned reading, (*b*) write a journal reflection, (*c*) write one question in the journal to ask in the group, and (*d*) bring the journal to the discussion.
2. The group develops a questionnaire that participants will use to assess themselves and one another.
3. At the conclusion of the discussion, participants fill out questionnaires about themselves. Then they fill out a questionnaire for each of the other group members.
4. Participants receive their assessments. For example, Gary gets questionnaires that others have filled out about him and his self-assessment. Each student presents a summary of the results at the next group meeting.
5. If the consensus is that a student is not prepared for discussion, a plan for improvement is developed. For example, if Gary is not taking the time to write in his journal, Paul can be assigned the task of reminding Gary to do so the day before the discussion. Or Louise can put a reminder card on Gary's desk that says "Don't forget to write in your journal. The next discussion is on Friday."

Usually, the group can suggest a plan for improvement. But sometimes you will need to develop the plan. If Gary is not doing the assigned reading, you need to determine the reason. Is Gary able to read the book? Is Gary spending too much time socializing? Is Gary's home life not conducive to quiet reading at home? These are questions related to professional and private issues, which the small group may not be qualified to answer.

Questionnaire for Assessing Preparation

Participant _____ Date _____

Assessor (if different from the participant): _____

• Did the student do the assigned reading?

    Yes   Don't Know   No

• Did the student write a journal reflection?

    Yes   No

• Did the student write at least one question in the journal?

    Yes   No

• Did the student bring the journal to the discussion?

    Yes   No

This questionnaire asks basic questions about students' level and quality of preparation for discussion.

Next Steps

If student assessment and your observation show that participants are not preparing for discussion, ask yourself the following:

◆ Did the students have access to the information?

◆ Was the information at the right level?

◆ Did I ensure that students had the necessary background knowledge?

◆ Did I ensure that the students had the necessary vocabulary?

Answering these questions may help you identify specific problems to address.

> See Chapters 3 and 4 for ways to engage students in and bring focus to their discussions.

FOCUS, PURPOSE, AND ENGAGEMENT

True discussions have a focus and a clear purpose. Participants may experience false starts and take side trips, but they have also identified a purpose for the discussion and strive to maintain focus to fulfill the purpose. They are engaged in the topic and committed to sharing information about it, learning from each other, and perhaps coming to some sort of a conclusion about it. In other words, the students own the discussion.

Your role is twofold: to identify focus and purpose for initial discussions and to show students how to develop their own purposes. The students' role is to monitor their discussion, drawing the group back to the focus if the discussion veers too far from the purpose.

Whereas you will typically look at individuals when assessing preparation, you will want to assess both individuals and the group as a whole for focus, purpose, and engagement. The standard should not be that all talk is about the topic. It won't be and shouldn't be. Students will naturally socialize some. If students think you expect them never to digress about the latest movie, they may provide you with "fake data" during assessment or may act in ways that don't reflect their usual behavior. (My colleagues and I [Day et al., 2002] found that one discussion group always turned off the tape recorder when they disagreed because somehow they thought disagreement was a bad thing!)

◆ Chitchat

◆ Discussing possible questions

◆ Identifying a question

◆ Focusing on the question

◆ Exploring other questions

◆ Identifying focus for next meeting

◆ Chitchat

Classroom Discussion

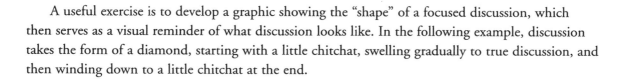

A useful exercise is to develop a graphic showing the "shape" of a focused discussion, which then serves as a visual reminder of what discussion looks like. In the following example, discussion takes the form of a diamond, starting with a little chitchat, swelling gradually to true discussion, and then winding down to a little chitchat at the end.

Assessing Focus, Purpose, and Engagement

Two simple strategies may be used for group self-assessment.

1. At the conclusion of each discussion, have each group respond in writing to two questions: *(a)* Did we identify one good question to discuss? and *(b)* What are three to five important points brought up in this discussion? Answering the first question helps students assess the degree to which they were focused, and answering the second question will also aid them in summarizing the discussion, discriminating big ideas from smaller ones, and clarifying those ideas. Rehearsing the discussion also moves the big ideas into long-term memory.
2. Appoint a Focus Assessor in each group. See guidelines below. (Use of this strategy usually assumes that all groups are meeting at the same time because the timer will be heard throughout the room.)

A third and more time-consuming strategy is to audiotape small-group discussions, have the participants listen to the tape, and ask them to critique the degree to which the group was focused. Kathleen Crawford and Theresa Hoopingarner (1993) used this strategy to great effect with first graders. Audiotaping is probably better than videotaping for this task because the students will not be distracted by how they look.

ACTIVITY

The Focus Assessor

1. Set a timer to ring every five minutes during small-group discussion time.
2. Every time the timer sounds, each group's appointed Focus Assessor writes a phrase that indicates what the group is discussing at that moment, such as "whether Paul [in *Hatchet*] should have...," "why some kids cheat on homework," or "the latest *Matrix* movie."
3. Near the end of the discussion, the Focus Assessor shares the list with the group. The group uses that information to decide if it was Mostly Focused, Somewhat Focused, or Poorly Focused. Having one person write down the focus avoids interrupting the discussion.

Next Steps

If students are having trouble keeping focused, setting purposes, or becoming engaged in discussion, you might concentrate on these questions:

◆ Does the class have criteria for good and bad questions?

◆ Do I model only good questions?

◆ Are my questions related to the curriculum, at the right level of difficulty, and engaging?

◆ Have I taught the students how to identify important ideas?

◆ Have I given the students strategies for monitoring their own discussions?

◆ Have I helped the class develop ownership of their discussions by scaffolding, probing, and listening?

◆ Do I ask the class to discuss for a variety of purposes, such as preparation for writing or reading or for follow-up?

◆ In whole-group discussion, do I invite participation by modeling good practices, involving all students, probing responses, keeping track of who participates, and listening? Do I model good body language?

INTERACTION

Successful discussion involves collaboration, active listening, respect, trust, and taking turns (which means knowing when to accept and give up the stage). Students must participate, take interest in what others have to say, seek clarification, and disagree courteously. In other words, their interaction must be healthy for true discussion to happen.

> Chapters 3 and 4 provide information about trust, taking turns, and other issues of participation.

Your job is to move students toward independence in whole-group and small-group discussions, through modeling, mini-lessons, and direct intervention when necessary. As with focus, purpose, and engagement, the students' jobs are to monitor the nature of the interactions in their discussions and to identify and solve (or get help solving) any problems.

Assessing Interaction

As for other aspects of discussion, the class should identify assessment questions for interaction. A list like this one may emerge:

1. Who talks a lot?

2. Who talks very little?

3. Do we listen to one another?

4. Do we follow up on others' comments?

5. Is the discussion civil?

Assessment of questions 1 and 2 can be accomplished by appointing a Tally Master or through the use of Talk Tokens. (See Chapter 4.) Questions 3 to 5 might be the responsibility of a group member in a new role, Miss Manners, who fills out a checklist like the one to the right during each discussion and then, at the end, leads the group in a short review of the data. Miss Manners records information for the group as a whole, not for each participant.

Miss Manners' Checklist

- Asked for more information ✓✓
- Added a detail to someone else's comment ✓✓ ✓
- Agreed with a comment ✓
- Disagreed politely with a comment ✓✓ ✓✓
- Disagreed impolitely with a comment ✓

Miss Manners' job is to keep track of group behavior and report results after the discussion.

Next Steps

If the assessment of interactions yield disappointing results, ask yourself:

◆ Do I model good listening?
◆ Do I model or use Think Alouds or mini-lessons to help students respond effectively to one another's comments?
◆ Have I taught the students strategies for taking turns?
◆ Have I formed appropriate groups?

LEVEL OF THINKING

Students are capable of high levels of thinking before, during, and after discussion. The trick is to get this to happen frequently so that it becomes the norm. The most effective discussions have both breadth and depth. Breadth is attained when the discussion is multidimensional—when participants explore more than one aspect of the topic or question. For example, discussion of whether *Stellaluna* (Cannon, 1993) is a good book should focus on more than the beautiful and informative illustrations. Depth occurs when discussion is more than superficial—when new information is brought to bear on the topic or question, comments are elaborated upon, subtopics introduced, clarification is sought, and ideas are challenged or supported. Discussions are more apt to be broad and deep when they take place across days and time is allowed for reflection and revision.

Chapter 3 explains how to select effective discussion questions. Chapter 5 provides information about using reflection to extend meaning.

You can guide the class to higher levels of thinking through judicious selection of topics and questions and through careful prompting, coaching, and scaffolding during whole-group work. Students must understand the difference between reporting and discussing and be committed to learning how to participate in extended, productive discussion. They must be willing to probe, extend, and graciously challenge one another's comments, and not move too quickly to terminate the discussion.

Assessing Level of Thinking

Assessing level of thinking is difficult. Adults, much less children, often have a hard time determining if they are dealing with big ideas and, if they decide they are, naming those ideas. The class may profit from a mini-lesson on identifying big ideas. Such a lesson has two purposes: to move students to higher levels of thinking and to prepare them to assess their own levels of thinking.

Once the students understand the concepts of big idea and little idea, they can begin to assess the level of discussion in their groups. One quick strategy for doing that is to have the group summarize their discussion by filling out a chart like the one to the right.

Another strategy is to have participants underline all big ideas in their journals before and after discussion. This increases the likelihood that big ideas will actually be addressed. Identifying the big ideas in journals after discussion also helps to secure those ideas in students' long-term memory.

> **Our Big Idea** _____
>
> The little ideas that led to the big idea
> 1.
>
> 2.
>
> 3.
>
> 4.

Charts like this one can help students understand the origin and development of their big ideas.

Next Steps

These questions can help you identify the source of problems with students' levels of thinking:

◆ Have I given the students time to revise meaning?

◆ Have I coached and scaffolded and celebrated revision of meaning?

◆ Have I avoided the IRE pattern?

◆ Have I taught the students how to seek and gain clarification of ideas?

◆ Have I taught the students how to identify big ideas and how to identify a chain of ideas?

Finding Big Ideas

Note: This is a variation of the mini-lesson called "Prioritizing for Assessment," which appears on page 115.

Objectives: To show students how little ideas add up to big ideas; to move the students to higher levels of thinking; to prepare them to assess their own levels of thinking.

Materials: Chalkboard, whiteboard, or chart paper; chalk or markers.

Steps:

1. Identify a question or topic for whole-class discussion, such as *Should bicycle riders be required to wear helmets?* **or** *Which is a better form of government, a democracy or a republic?*
2. As the class discusses the question, write down key phrases or points as they are introduced. On the board, cluster ideas that somehow fit together. (See Figure 6-1.)
3. When discussion slows down, direct the students' attention to the board. Ask them to provide a label for the big idea of each cluster. Model the strategy for identifying a big idea through a Think Aloud using two clusters, one that will be somewhat easy for the students to identify and one that will be somewhat difficult. This discussion may provoke more big ideas. If it does, add the ideas to the board. If a little idea never contributes to a big idea, the class needs to decide if it is a big idea by itself or simply an extraneous little idea. For example, "Government should stay out of personal business" may be identified as a big idea in itself and may provoke further discussion. "It's wimpy" may be judged as not leading to a big idea and, therefore, not critical to the discussion.

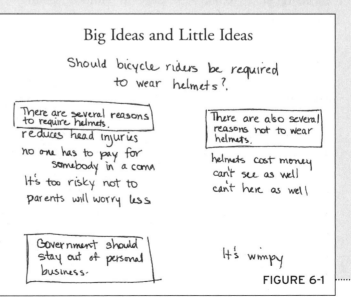

Big Ideas and Little Ideas

Should bicycle riders be required to wear helmets?.

There are several reasons to require helmets.
reduces head injuries
no one has to pay for somebody in a coma
It's too risky not to
parents will worry less

There are also several reasons not to wear helmets.
helmets cost money
can't see as well
can't here as well

Government should stay out of personal business.

It's wimpy

FIGURE 6-1

What Have Students Learned Through Discussion?

In Chapters 1 and 2, I proposed that discussion is not an end in itself. It is a means to learning. So, in order to determine if discussion has been successful, it is important to assess what students have learned as a result of the discussion. What do they know after the discussion that they didn't know before? This can be assessed according to the new meanings students gain and the accuracy of those meanings.

NEW MEANING

Discussion provides the opportunity for new meaning to emerge as a result of collaborating with peers and sharing perspectives. As participants struggle to express their ideas, they clarify and often change those ideas. Further, they listen, adding information to what they already know and viewing the topic or question from other participants' perspectives. They expect to leave the discussion with a different understanding and continue to revisit and refine their thinking.

Assessing New Meaning

The strategies for assessing level of thinking (page 124) will also help students uncover what they have learned. In addition, students can use strategies from earlier chapters, such as the Discussion Planning Sheet (Chapter 3, page 83, and Appendix 6) which reveals facts, opinions, conclusions, and new thoughts that students gain after discussion. The Continuing Thinking After Discussion chart (Chapter 5, pages 102–103, and Appendix 7) and the Tracking My Thinking chart (Chapter 5, page 108, and Appendix 9) both provide a record of the new ideas students form in discussion.

Next Steps

If assessment shows that the students are struggling to make meaning in discussions, ask yourself:
◆ Have I taught the students how to seek and gain clarification of ideas?
◆ Do I model good listening?
◆ Have I coached and scaffolded and celebrated revision of meaning?
◆ Have I taught the students how to identify big ideas and how to identify a chain of ideas?

ACCURATE MEANING

Accuracy of meaning is important, especially in the content areas. A discussion that concludes that humans have never landed on the moon or that Degas was strongly influenced by Egyptian sculpture is not a successful discussion! Assessment of discussion, therefore, must ascertain to some degree the validity of the meaning constructed.

Assessing Accuracy of Meaning

Assessment of the accuracy of ideas is difficult. Students may think their ideas are accurate, but they may be inaccurate in their assessment! However, they should be able to state their ideas clearly and, from there, assess how confident they are about them. After all, knowing what you think is a precursor for assessing the accuracy of what you think. The Confidence Rating activity described in Chapter 2 (pages 43–44) can assist students in thinking about the probable accuracy of their ideas. Similarly, the Determining if Clarification Is Needed strategy described in Chapter 4 (page 97) can lead students to think deeply about their ideas and, in the process, discover inaccurate information.

Next Steps

If your students are not attending to accuracy, ask yourself, "Have I modeled 'truth in discussion' responses?" Pointing out when students use the right logic but base their thinking on wrong information will help them remember their responsibility for accuracy. (See Chapter 2 for details.)

Record Keeping

The record keeping associated with assessment can easily become burdensome. But if you don't keep good records, what's the point of assessment? You assess in order to determine if your students are learning, to intervene as needed, and to improve your program. So the time it takes to keep good records is time well spent.

Start by creating a discussion folder for each student in which you will gather assessments and work samples. A simple way to keep track of each student's progress is to staple a Discussion Goals Checklist inside the front cover of each student's discussion folder. (See Appendix 12.) As you gather information through group- and self-assessments and through your own observations and use of rubrics, place these papers in students' folders and check off the results on the checklist. Then periodically use the student checklists to determine how well you are meeting your goals.

Final Thought

Because developing discussion skills takes time out of an already crowded six-hour school day, assessing the effects of discussion on learning the curriculum is absolutely critical. Think both big and small! Think big when it comes to your goals, but think small when it comes to the steps to reach those goals. Identify small monthly goals, assess your students' progress, tinker with your curriculum, and celebrate even the smallest strides toward reaching your big goals. You will find that discussion is an exciting tool for engaging your students in learning. Give your students and yourself the time you need to make true discussion an everyday event in your classroom.

Appendices

Appendix 1: Discussion Web 130

Appendix 2: Listening In on Discussion Form 131

Appendix 3: Confidence Rating Form 132

Appendix 4: Vocabulary Expectations Chart 133

Appendix 5: Planning Chart for Whole-Class Discussion 134

Appendix 6: Discussion Planning Sheet 135

Appendix 7: Continuing Thinking After Discussion 136

Appendix 8: Analyzing Reflection Journal Entries 137

Appendix 9: Tracking My Thinking 138

Appendix 10: Rubric: Postdiscussion Journal Entries 139

Appendix 11: Determining if You Have a Discussion Curriculum in Place 140

Appendix 12: Discussion Goals Checklist 141

Appendix 13: Plan for a Teacher Workshop Based on This Book 143

Appendix 1
Discussion Web

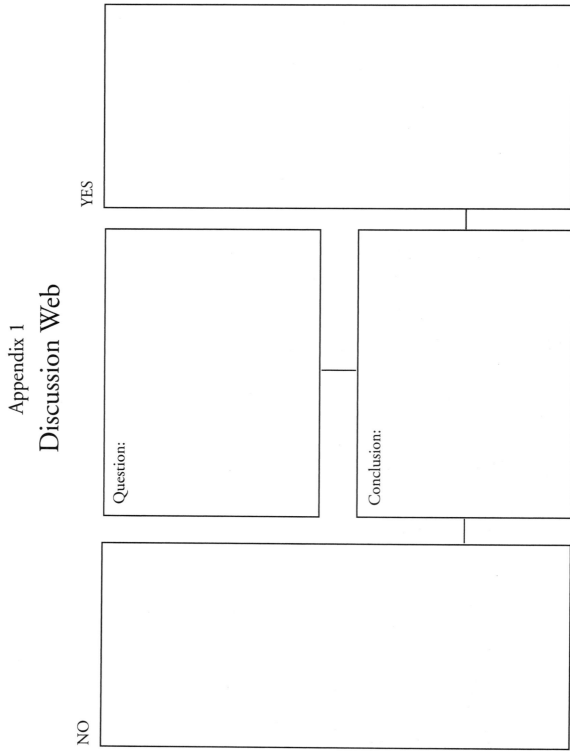

YES

Question:

Conclusion:

NO

An explanation of how to use this reproducible appears on pages 32–33.

Appendix 2

Listening In on Discussion Form

Date: _____ **Participants:** _____

Focus of Discussion:

How did the discussion start?

❑ I gave an assignment to discuss.

My purpose:

❑ I asked a question.

Did I intend this to provoke a discussion or just to get an answer?

❑ _____ asked a question.

❑ Other:

What was the purpose of the discussion?

An explanation of how to use this reproducible appears on page 34.

Appendix 3

Confidence Rating Form

Information Leading to Our Conclusion	Confidence Rating

An explanation of how to use this reproducible appears on pages 43–44.

Appendix 4

Vocabulary Expectations Chart

Word	Recognize and have meaning	Have word recognition	Won't know at all

An explanation of how to use this reproducible appears on page 62.

from *Classroom Discussion* by Dixie Lee Spiegel, © 2005, Scholastic Professional Books

Planning Chart for Whole-Class Discussion

Essential Background Knowledge

Essential Vocabulary

Goals/Purposes

An explanation of how to use this reproducible appears on page 66.

from *Classroom Discussion* by Dixie Lee Spiegel, © 2005, Scholastic Professional Books

Appendix 6

Discussion Planning Sheet

Name _____ **Date** _____

Question or Topic:

Facts	Opinions	Conclusions	New Thoughts After Discussion

An explanation of how to use this reproducible appears on page 83.

from *Classroom Discussion* by Dixie Lee Spiegel, © 2005, Scholastic Professional Books

Continuing Thinking After Discussion

What I Originally Thought	New Information From Others	What I Think Now

An explanation of how to use this reproducible appears on pages 102–103.

Appendix 8

Analyzing Reflection Journal Entries

Date	Aha!	Yes, I Can See	Hmm, but No, Thanks	No Reflection

3 _____

2 _____

1 _____

Aha!	Yes, I Can See	Hmm, but No, Thanks	No Reflection

An explanation of how to use this reproducible appears on pages 106–107.

from *Classroom Discussion* by Dixie Lee Spiegel, © 2005, Scholastic Professional Books

Tracking My Thinking

My Original Idea	What Others Thought	What I Think Now
Big Idea **Support** **Support**		

An explanation of how to use this reproducible appears on page 108.

Appendix 10

Rubric: Postdiscussion Journal Entries

The student's skill in writing postdiscussion reflections is:

Well Developed	Developing	Poorly Developed
Writes in journal after discussion; entry shows evidence of reflection, e.g., consideration of other points of view, extension of ideas, supported confirmation of original ideas	Writes in journal after discussion; entry lacks evidence of reflection, e.g., consideration of other points of view, extension of ideas, supported confirmation of original ideas	Does not write in journal or the entry is very short and generic, e.g., "I liked the book."

Comments:

An explanation of how to use this reproducible appears on pages 111–112.

Appendix 11

Determining if You Have a Discussion Curriculum in Place

Each student will be able to:

Start Off Discussion

❑ come to discussion prepared

❑ pose interesting questions and set purposes

Participate

❑ contribute to discussion

❑ listen to others

❑ take turns

❑ respond to others' comments

❑ ask for clarification when needed

❑ disagree civilly

❑ be open to new ideas

❑ gain new information from discussion

❑ stay focused

❑ sustain discussion so that some degree of depth is reached

Think and Reflect

❑ reach high levels of thinking

❑ continue to reflect and revise thinking after discussion has ended

Background information for using this reproducible appears on page 117.

from *Classroom Discussion* by Dixie Lee Spiegel, © 2005, Scholastic Professional Books

Discussion Goals Checklist

Name: _____

Preparation

❑ Gathers input through reading/viewing/listening. (Circle appropriate choice.)

Date _____ *Score* WELL DEVELOPED DEVELOPING POORLY DEVELOPED

❑ Comes to the discussion with questions, journal entries, and other evidence of inquiry.

Date _____ *Score* WELL DEVELOPED DEVELOPING POORLY DEVELOPED

Focus, Purpose, and Engagement

❑ Sets purposes for discussion.

Date _____ *Score* WELL DEVELOPED DEVELOPING POORLY DEVELOPED

❑ Identifies important ideas discussed.

Date _____ *Score* WELL DEVELOPED DEVELOPING POORLY DEVELOPED

❑ Reflects after discussion.

Date _____ *Score* WELL DEVELOPED DEVELOPING POORLY DEVELOPED

Interaction

❑ Listens to others.

Date _____ *Score* WELL DEVELOPED DEVELOPING POORLY DEVELOPED

❑ Probes others' responses, seeks clarification, elaborates, agrees, disagrees.

Date _____ *Score* WELL DEVELOPED DEVELOPING POORLY DEVELOPED

❑ Shows respect for others, trusts others, and interacts with civility.

Date _____ *Score* WELL DEVELOPED   DEVELOPING   POORLY DEVELOPED

❑ Participates an appropriate amount. Takes turns.

Date _____ *Score* WELL DEVELOPED   DEVELOPING   POORLY DEVELOPED

Level of Thinking

❑ Revises ideas through discussion.

Date _____ *Score* WELL DEVELOPED   DEVELOPING   POORLY DEVELOPED

❑ Probes, challenges, and expands upon others' ideas.

Date _____ *Score* WELL DEVELOPED   DEVELOPING   POORLY DEVELOPED

❑ Identifies big ideas and the ideas that support the big ideas.

Date _____ *Score* WELL DEVELOPED   DEVELOPING   POORLY DEVELOPED

What Students Have Learned: New Meaning

❑ Collaborates in creating new meaning.

Date _____ *Score* WELL DEVELOPED   DEVELOPING   POORLY DEVELOPED

❑ Can chart the path of developing ideas.

Date _____ *Score* WELL DEVELOPED   DEVELOPING   POORLY DEVELOPED

What Students Have Learned: Accurate Meaning

❑ Can identify own level of confidence about ideas.

Date _____ *Score* WELL DEVELOPED   DEVELOPING   POORLY DEVELOPED

Background information for using this reproducible appears on pages 118–127.

from *Classroom Discussion* by Dixie Lee Spiegel, © 2005, Scholastic Professional Books

Appendix 13

Plan for a Teacher Workshop Based on This Book

One important way to use this book is to discuss the ideas in it! So I have designed this inservice plan for you and your colleagues to help promote discussion in your classrooms. The plan is detailed so that you can implement it without outside help. You and your colleagues can share the role of leader or one person can assume that role. Hopefully, your school district will provide you with Continuing Education Units (CEUs) for completing this plan. Be sure all activities within the plan are considered for CEU credit.

The plan is made up of four two-hour meetings plus time for reading chapters in this book and carrying out classroom-based "homework" assignments. Meetings might take place twice in the fall and twice in the spring, with time between sessions for you to try out ideas. The plan assumes that participants teach at several grade levels, but it can be easily adapted for participants who teach at the same grade level. Because there is so much small-group discussion, it can be used with groups as large as 50, although about 25 participants is ideal.

Each session is divided into five sections:

◆ **Preparation by the Participants** explains what group members need to do before coming to the session. You have chapters to read from the book and, after the first session, homework that should be completed. If you come to the session without this preparation, you will not gain much from the inservice.

◆ **Workshop Leader's Materials** lists what the designated leader needs to bring to the session.

◆ **Goals** suggest purposes and aims for each session.

◆ **Suggested Outlines** present activities designed to help you meet the goals. They are "lesson plans" of sorts. As with all lesson plans, you should adjust them as you go, giving more time to some activities, eliminating some altogether if you determine the group does not need them, and adding other activities. The outlines are bases from which to start.

◆ **Homework** recommends classroom-based activities to prepare for the next session. You may choose activities other than the suggested ones, but for this plan to be meaningful, alternatives must require participants to try out discussion strategies between sessions.

Session 1:
What Is Discussion? Why Is It Important? and
What Is My Attitude About Using It in My Classroom?

Preparation by the Participants

1. Read Chapters 1 and 2 of this book.

2. Try the Listening In activity on page 34. Bring your draft of a discussion checklist (described in "Listening In" on page 13) to class.

3. Always bring your book to the sessions. You may need to refer to it.

Workshop Leader's Materials

Chart paper, markers, masking tape

Goals of Session 1

1. To develop a commitment to use discussion in the classroom

   a) To reflect upon personal attitudes toward using discussion

   b) To explore the benefits of discussion

2. To seek solutions for barriers to effective discussion

3. To explore the nature of true discussion

4. To prepare for effective discussion in the classroom

5. To practice effective discussion strategies

Suggested Outline

The Workshop Leader may do the following:

1. Make introductions as needed, provide an overview, and explain the expectations for successful completion of the inservice and earning CEUs. (15 minutes)

2. Have a U-Debate (see page 67) to explore attitudes toward discussion in participants' classrooms, addressing goals 1, 2, and 5 above. (30 minutes)

   ◆ Have participants do quick writes (page 97), jotting down how they feel about using discussion in their classes. To indicate their initial attitudes toward using discussion in their classrooms, ask participants to rate themselves on a scale of 0 (most negative) to 10 (most positive). (3 minutes)

◆ Seat participants according to their assessment of their attitudes. Make a quick tally of the ratings. (2 minutes)

◆ Discuss the benefits of and barriers to discussion and possible ways to overcome the barriers. (20 minutes)

◆ Have participants change seats as their attitudes change per the U-Debate format.

◆ Have everyone quick write a second time, reflecting on how their attitudes changed during the discussion and rating themselves again. Make a tally of the second ratings and use this information to plan the next three sessions. (5 minutes)

3. Explore the nature of true discussion, addressing goals 2, 4, and 5 above. (20 minutes)

◆ Have participants meet in small groups to discuss and combine checklists that they generated for the Listening In activity. Have them combine lists into one comprehensive list divided into "essential" and "desirable" characteristics of a true discussion. (15 minutes)

◆ Ask each group to share its checklist with the entire group. Develop a class chart labeled True Discussion. (Note: You will need to provide a copy of the chart to each participant shortly after Session 1, for use on homework assignment 2, below.) (5 minutes)

4. Develop a set of discussion questions to help students reach a curricular goal, addressing goals 4 and 5 above. (30 minutes)

◆ Organize participants into grade-level groups and have them develop a set of sequenced questions to help students reach one curricular goal, following the models on pages 25 and 26. The participants might use the sections on Getting Discussion Started in the different disciplines (Chapter 2) to help select appropriate questions. Each participant should leave the group ready to use the questions in her classroom. (See homework assignment 2, below.)

Homework

1. Read Chapter 3 of this book.

2. Before the next inservice session, provide time for discussion in your classroom, following the guidelines on pages 39–41. You will probably wish to combine this activity with assignment 3, below. Be prepared to discuss your experiences in Session 2.

3. With your students, use the sequenced set of discussion questions developed in Session 1. Use the class chart on True Discussion from activity 3 to evaluate how well the discussion went. Bring the chart to class.

4. Have your students do at least one of the following activities. For the activity they choose, write

up a "lesson plan" to show how you prepared for the activity, developed it, and followed up. In addition, reflect in writing on what went well and what didn't. Be prepared to discuss your plan during the next session.

◆ Form at least one Buzz Group (page 31).

◆ Have your students complete a Discussion Web (pages 32–33).

◆ Do the Listening In activity on page 34.

◆ Initiate a discussion using the Semantic Webbing activity (page 49).

◆ Try out the Fishbowl technique for discussion (page 51).

◆ Use Response Journals to prepare for discussion (page 55).

Session 2: Preparing for Discussion

Preparation by the Participants

1. Do the four homework assignments from Session 1.

2. Bring your curriculum guides, standard course of study, or other documents describing the curriculum for your grade level.

3. Always bring your book to the sessions.

Workshop Leader's Materials

True Discussion chart from Session 1, chart paper, markers, masking tape

Goals of Session 2

1. To reflect upon the discussion strategies from Session 1, homework assignment 3, which asked participants to identify issues and solutions to problems

2. To continue to reflect upon the nature of True Discussion

3. To collaborate on ways to prepare the classroom climate for discussion

4. To practice writing good questions for discussion

5. To practice effective discussion strategies

Appendix 13 • Page 5

Suggested Outline

The Workshop Leader may do the following:

1. Have participants reintroduce themselves if needed and provide an overview of Session 2. (5 minutes)
2. Discuss the activities participants used for homework assignment 4, addressing goals 1 and 5. (25 minutes)
    ◆ Divide participants into small groups according to which homework activity they completed. (Those who tried Fishbowl work together, those who tried Buzz Groups work together, and so on.) Have each group discuss what worked well and what problems they encountered. (15 minutes)
    ◆ Use the jigsaw procedures (page 81) to form new groups made up of one member from each of the first groups. Members of the second groups report to each other the results of the first discussion. In this way those who did not try an activity will learn its benefits and potential problems. (10 minutes)

3. Revise the True Discussion chart based on what the participants have learned about discussion since the last session, addressing goal 2. (5 minutes)
4. Collaborate on ways to prepare the classroom climate for discussion, addressing goals 3 and 5. (40 minutes)
    ◆ Have participants select one of the following goals: (1) creating a spirit of inquiry, (2) developing teacher trust of students, (3) developing student trust of the teacher, (4) promoting student trust of peers, or (5) enhancing student trust of self. Reorganize groups according to goals and have participants identify several guidelines for reaching these goals in their classrooms. Write the guidelines on a chart and make copies for the participants. (30 minutes)
    ◆ Ask each group to share its chart. (10 minutes)
5. Write questions for a curriculum topic, addressing goal 4. (35 minutes)
    ◆ Divide participants into grade-level groups and have each group identify one curriculum goal and follow the steps on pages 77–79 to write an application-level question and a set of prep questions, addressing goal 4. (35 minutes)

    Hint: After the group identifies a curriculum goal, each participant may write an application-level question to propose to the group. In this way each participant brings something to the discussion. Similarly, after one application-level question is selected, each participant may write several prep questions and share them.

Homework

1. Read Chapters 4 and 5 of this book.

2. Use the grouping strategies from pages 71–77 to form small discussion groups. Be prepared to discuss any problems and successes you encounter.

3. Have your students do activities from at least two categories, below. For each activity bring a one-paragraph reflection about the experience to the next session.

- ◆ **Preparation**

     Background Knowledge Quiz (page 60)

     List-Group-Label (page 61)

     Exclusion Brainstorming (page 63)

     Expectation Outline (page 64)

     K-W-L Strategy (page 65)

     Planning Chart for Whole-Class Discussion (page 66 and Appendix 5)

- ◆ **Follow-Up**

     U-Debate Forum (page 67)

- ◆ **Preparing Students**

     Putting It All Together (page 81)

     Journals (pages 82–83)

     Discussion Planning Sheet (page 83 and Appendix 6)

     Developing Guidelines for Discussion (pages 83–84)

Session 3: Facilitating and Following Up on Discussion

Preparation by the Participants

1. Complete the three homework assignments from Session 2.

2. Always bring this book to the sessions.

Workshop Leader's Materials

Chart paper, markers, masking tape, one blank Discussion Web for each participant (Appendix 1)

Goals of Session 3

1. To explore participants' experiences with grouping
2. To explore participants' experiences with preparing students for discussion
3. To provide participants an opportunity to initiate discussion and get answers to their questions
4. To practice strategies to facilitate discussion

Suggested Outline

The Workshop Leader may do the following:

1. Have participants reintroduce themselves as necessary and provide an overview of the session. (5 minutes)
2. Share experiences with grouping, addressing goal 1 (homework assignment 2 from Session 2). (30 minutes)
   ◆ On a chart, list grouping problems along with solutions. Make copies for the participants. Hint: The Workshop Leader might want to use the List-Group-Label strategy (page 61) for this discussion, which will help participants focus on big ideas rather than isolated problems.
3. Share reflections on preparing for and following up discussion, addressing goal 2 (homework assignment 3 from Session 2). (20 minutes)
   ◆ Divide participants into groups according to the activities they completed. Have each group use Steps 1–3 of Discussion Webs (pages 32–33) to determine whether the activity was effective or not. (Note: Although the activity is usually done in pairs, it can also be done in small groups.) (10 minutes)
   ◆ Post the webs around the room and give participants the opportunity to read each one. (10 minutes)
4. Ask the participants if they have questions or concerns about discussion that have not yet been dealt with in the workshop. Engage the participants in a whole-group discussion of these questions, addressing goal 3. (30 minutes)
5. Practice strategies for facilitating discussion, addressing goal 4. (25 minutes)
   ◆ Divide participants into small groups and tell them that they are going to engage in a discussion based on a relevant question that you give them. Assign the same question to all groups, or have a different question for each group. For example, the school may be considering new policies, or there may be specific grade-level issues that need exploration.
   ◆ Assign participants roles and have them review their roles (5 minutes):

- Tally Master (page 91)
- Discussion Leader (page 92)
- Connector-Extender (page 95)
- Clarifier (pages 95–96)

◆ Have each group discuss the assigned question. (15 minutes)

◆ Have the group then talk about the effectiveness of the assigned roles for facilitating discussion. (5 minutes)

Homework

1. Read Chapter 6 of this book.
2. Have your students do at least one of the following activities. Reflect in writing on what went well and what didn't. Be prepared to discuss your activity in class.
   - Semantic Webbing (page 97)
   - Mini-Lesson on Shaping an Idea (page 98–99)
   - Mini-Lesson on Continuing Thinking After Discussion (pages 102–103)
   - Reflection Journals (pages 104–107)
   - Thinking Charts (page 108)

Session 4: Assessing Discussion

Preparation by the Participants

1. Do the two homework assignments from Session 3.
2. Always bring your book to the sessions.

Workshop Leader's Materials

Chart paper, markers, masking tape

Goals of Session 4

1. To explore participants' experiences with facilitating discussion
2. To discuss a discussion curriculum and design assessments

Appendix 13 • Page 9

3. To provide participants an opportunity to make rubrics for assessment
4. To provide participants an opportunity to initiate discussion and get answers to their questions
5. To practice strategies for facilitating discussion

Suggested Outline

The Workshop Leader may do the following:

1. Explore participants' experiences with facilitating discussion (homework assignment 2 from Session 3). (35 minutes)
   - ◆ Divide participants into small groups according to the activities they completed for homework and have them answer the questions "What was the greatest benefit of this activity" and "What was the greatest drawback?" (15 minutes)
   - ◆ As a whole group, use Semantic Webbing (page 97) to create two charts, one for benefits and one for drawbacks. Start by having each group share their discussion points, but allow additional information. Be sure to cluster the ideas into larger concepts, as specified in the webbing guidelines. (20 minutes)
2. Discuss a discussion curriculum and design assessments, addressing goals 2 and 3. (60 minutes)
   - ◆ As a whole group, explore the Discussion Goals Checklist (Appendix 12). Have the participants add or delete goals as they see fit. (15 minutes)
   - ◆ Discuss the qualities of an effective rubric for assessment. (5 minutes)
   - ◆ Divide participants into grade-level groups to prepare an assessment rubric for one major category listed on pages 118–123 (Preparation, Focus, Purpose, and Engagement, etc.). For example, third-grade teachers might prepare an assessment for Interactions while fifth-grade teachers might focus on Levels of Thinking, since, presumably, their students are more sophisticated readers.
   - ◆ Collect and photocopy the rubrics and distribute them to all participants. (5 minutes)
3. Discuss topics initiated by the participants. Ask if they have questions or concerns about discussion that have not been dealt with in the workshop. Engage the participants in a whole-group discussion of these questions, addressing goal 3. (25 minutes)

References
Children's Literature Cited

Armstrong, W. (1969). *Sounder*. New York: HarperCollins.

Bunting, E. (1993). *Terrible things*. Philadelphia: The Jewish Publication Society.

Byars, B. (1993). *The pinballs*. New York: HarperCollins.

Byars, B. (1996). *Cracker Jackson*. New York: Penguin Putnam.

Cannon, J. (1993). *Stellaluna*. San Diego: Harcourt Brace.

Coerr, E. (1977). *Sadako and the thousand paper cranes*. New York: Putnam.

Cushman, K. (1995). *The midwife's apprentice*. New York: HarperCollins.

Gipson, F. (1956). *Old Yeller*. New York: Harper & Row.

Lee, H. (1960). *To kill a mockingbird*. Philadelphia: Lippincott.

L'Engle, M. (1962). *A wrinkle in time*. New York: Farrar, Straus and Giroux.

Lewis, C. S. (1950). *The lion, the witch, and the wardrobe*. New York: HarperCollins.

Paulsen, G. (1987). *Hatchet*. New York: Puffin Books.

Rawls, W. (1961). *Where the red fern grows*. New York: Doubleday.

Seuss, D. (1938). *The 500 hats of Bartholomew Cubbins*. New York: Vanguard Press.

Silverstein, S. (1974). "Sick." In *Where the sidewalk ends* (pp. 58–59). New York: Harper and Row.

Taylor, M. (1976). *Roll of thunder, hear my cry*. New York: Puffin Books.

Van Allsburg, C. (1991). *The wretched stone*. Boston: Houghton Mifflin.

Viorst, J. (1971). *The tenth good thing about Barney*. New York: Atheneum.

References
Professional Literature Cited

Allan, K., & Miller, M. (2000). *Literacy and learning: Strategies for middle and secondary schools*. Boston: Houghton Mifflin.

Almasi, J. F. (1995). The nature of fourth graders' socio-cognitive conflicts in peer-led and teacher-led discussions of literature. *Reading Research Quarterly, 30* (3), 314–351.

Almasi, J. F., & Gambrell, L. (1994). Socio-cognitive conflict in peer-led and teacher-led discussions of literature. *Reading Research Report #12*, Athens, GA: National Reading Research Center.

Alvermann, D. (1991). The discussion web: A graphic aid for learning across the curriculum. *Reading Teacher, 45*, 92–99.

Alvermann, D., Swafford, J., & Montero, M. (2004). *Content area literacy instruction: Elementary grades*. Boston: Pearson Education, Inc.

Alvermann, D., Young, J., Weaver, D., Hinchman, K., Moore, D., Phelps, S., et al. (1996). Middle and high school students' perceptions of how they experience text-based discussions: A multicase study. *Reading Research Quarterly, 31* (3), 244–267.

Anzul, M. (1993). Exploring literature with children within a transactional framework. In K. Holland, R. Hungerford, & S. Ernst (Eds.), *Journeying: Children respond to literature* (pp. 187–203). Portsmouth, NH: Heinemann.

Athanases, S. (1998). Developing a classroom community of interpreters. *English Journal, 77*, 45–48.

Bahktin, M. (1981). *Speech genres and other late essays* (C. Emerson & M. Holquist, Trans.). Austin, TX: University of Texas Press.

Baloche, L., Mauger, M., Willis, T., Filinuk, H., & Michalsky, B. (1993). Fishbowls, creative controversy, talking chips: Exploring literature cooperatively. *English Journal, 82*, 43–48.

Billings, L., & Fitzgerald, J. (2002). Dialogic discussion and the Paedeia seminar. *American Educational Research Journal, 39*, 907–941.

Blachowicz, C. (1986). Making connections: Alternatives to the vocabulary notebook. *Journal of Reading, 29*, 43–49.

Bloom, B. (Ed.) (1956). *Taxonomy of educational objectives*. New York: Longman.

Bloome, D., & Green, J. (1992). Educational contexts of literacy. In W. A. Grabe (Ed.), *Annual Review of Applied Linguistics, 12,* 49–70. New York: Cambridge University Press.

Brumbaugh, D., & Rock, D. (2001). *Teaching secondary mathematics* (2nd ed.). Mahwah, NJ: Lawrence Erlbaum Associates.

Chase, N., & Hynd, C. (1987). Reader response: An alternative way to teach students to think about text. *Journal of Reading, 20,* 530–540.

Cox, C., & Many, J. (1992). Toward an understanding of the aesthetic response to literature. *Language Arts, 69,* 28–33.

Crawford, K., & Hoopingarner, T. (1993). A kaleidoscope of conversation: A case study of a first-grade literature group. In K. Pierce and C. Gilles (Eds.), *Cycles of meaning* (pp. 261–273). Portsmouth, NH: Heinemann.

Daniels, H. (2002). *Literature circles: Voice and choice in book clubs and reading groups.* Portland, ME: Stenhouse.

Davies, B., & Harré, R. (1990). Positioning: The discursive production of selves. *Journal for the Theory of Social Behavior, 20,* 43–63.

Day, J. P., Spiegel, D. L., McLellan, J., & Brown, V. B. (2002). *Moving forward with literature circles.* New York: Scholastic Inc.

Dynneson, T., & Gross, R. (1995). *Designing effective instruction for secondary social studies.* Englewood Cliffs, NJ: Merrill.

Ellis, S., & Whalen, S. (1990). *Cooperative learning: Getting started.* Jefferson City, MO: Scholastic Inc.

Freedman, L. (1993). Teacher talk: The role of the teacher in literature discussion groups. In K. Pierce and C. Gilles (Eds.), *Cycles of meaning* (pp. 219–235). Portsmouth, NH: Heinemann.

Freedman, G., & Reynolds, E. (1980). Enriching basal reader lessons with semantic webbing. *Reading Teacher, 33,* 677–684.

Fuhler, C. (1994). Response journals: Just one more time with feeling. *Journal of Reading, 37,* 400–405.

Gilles, C. (1993). We make an idea: Cycles of meaning in literature discussion groups. In K. Pierce and C. Gilles (Eds.), *Cycles of meaning* (pp. 199–217). Portsmouth, NH: Heinemann.

Graham, M., & Spiegel, D. (1996). Prompts for different purposes. Unpublished manuscript.

Guthrie, J., Van Meter, P., McCann, A., Wigfield, A., Bennett, L., Poundstone, C., et al. (1996). Growth of literacy engagement: Changes in motivations and strategies during concept-oriented reading instruction. *Reading Research Quarterly, 31,* 306–322.

Harste, J. (1993). Inquiry-based instruction. *Primary Voices K–6, 1*, 2–5.

Harste, J., & Short, K., with Burke, C. (1988). *Creating classrooms for authors: The reading-writing connection.* Portsmouth, NH: Heinemann.

Jacque, D. (1993). The judge comes to kindergarten. In K. Holland, R. Hungerford, & S. Ernst (Eds.), *Journeying: Children respond to literature* (pp. 43–53). Portsmouth, NH: Heinemann.

Jarolimeck, J. (1986). *Social studies in elementary education* (7th ed.). New York: Macmillan.

Langer, J. A. (1992). Rethinking literature instruction. In J. A. Langer (Ed.), *Literature instruction: A focus on student response* (pp. 35–53). Washington, DC: National Council of Teachers of English.

Leal, D. (1993). The power of literacy peer-group discussions: How children collaboratively negotiate meaning. *Reading Teacher, 47*, 114–120.

Lemke, J. L. (1990). *Talking science: Language, learning, and values.* Norwood, NJ: Ablex.

Many, J., & Wiseman, D. (1992). Analyzing versus experiencing the effects of teaching approaches on students' responses. In J. Many & C. Cox (Eds.), *Reader stance and literary understanding* (pp. 250–276). Norwood, NJ: Ablex.

McMahon, S. (1994). Student-led book clubs: Traversing a river of interpretation. *The New Advocate, 7*, 109–125.

Mercer, N. (1995). *The guided construction of knowledge: Talk amongst teachers and learners.* Philadelphia, PA: Multilingual Matters Ltd.

Nystrand, M., & Gamoran, A. (1991). Instructional discourse, student engagement, and literature achievement. *Research in the Teaching of English, 25*, 261–290.

Nystrand, M., & Gamoran, A. (1993). From discourse communities to interpretive communities. In G. Newell & R. Durst (Eds.), *Exploring texts: The role of discussion and writing in the teaching and learning of literature* (pp. 91–111). Norwood, MA: Christopher Gordon.

Ogle, D. (1986). K-W-L: A teaching model that develops active reading of expository text. *Reading Teacher, 39*, 564–570.

Peterson, R., & Eeds, M. (1990). *Grand conversations: Literature groups in action.* Richmond Hill, ONT: Scholastic Canada Ltd.

Pierce, K., & Gilles, C. (Eds.), (1993). *Cycles of meaning: Exploring the potential of talk in learning communities.* Portsmouth, NH: Heinemann.

Professional Standards for Teaching Mathematics (1991). Reston, VA: National Council of Teachers of Mathematics.

Richards, I. A. (1942). *How to read a page.* Boston: Beacon Press.

Rosenblatt, L. (1978). *The Reader, the text, the poem: The transactional theory of the literary work.* Carbondale, IL: Southern Illinois University Press.

Sheppard, L. (1990). Our class knows Frog and Toad. In K. Short & K. Pierce (Eds.), *Talking about books: Creating literate communities* (pp. 71–81). Portsmouth, NH: Heinemann.

Short, K. (1993). Making connections across literature and life. In K. Holland, R. Hungerford, & S. Ernst (Eds.), *Journeying: Children responding to literature* (pp. 284–301). Portsmouth, NH: Heinemann.

Spiegel, D. (1981). Six alternatives to the Directed Reading Activity. *The Reading Teacher, 34,* 914–920.

Spiegel, D. (1996). The role of trust in reader-response groups. *Language Arts, 73,* 332–339.

Taba, H. (1967). *Teacher's handbook for elementary social studies.* Reading, MA: Addison-Wesley.

Trowbridge, L., Bybee, R., & Powell, J. (2000). *Teaching secondary science.* Upper Saddle River, NJ: Prentice-Hall.

Turner, J., & Paris, S. (1995). How literacy tasks influence children's motivation for literacy. *Reading Teacher, 48,* 662–673.

Vygotsky, L. (1978). *Mind in society: The development of higher psychological processes.* Cambridge, MA: Harvard University Press.

Wrubel, R. M. (2002). *Great grouping strategies.* New York: Scholastic Inc.

Index

A

activities
  background knowledge quiz, 60
  boiling water in a paper cup, 46–47
  Buzz Groups, 31
  Consult the Class, 72
  discussion webs, 32–33
  exclusion brainstorming, 63
  expectation outline, 64
  Fishbowl, 51
  Focus Assessor, 121
  K-W-L strategy, 65
  List-Group-Label, 61
  Listening In, 13, 34, 53, 73, 78, 111
  Pick Your Spot, 73
  Putting It All Together, 81
  response journals, 56
  semantic webbing, 49, 97
  U-Debate forum, 67
Allan, Karen, 73
Almasi, Janice, 14–15, 17, 24–25, 88
Alvermann, Donna, 70–71, 74, 77–78, 88
Anzul, Margaret, 19
application-level questions, 77
Armstrong, W., *Sounder*, 50
arts discussions, 53–56
  cultural, contextual influences and, 55–56
  personal connections and, 53–55
assessment
  discussion curriculum and, 109–110
  focus, purpose, engagement, 120–121
  guidelines, 114–115
  how to perform, 111–112
  interaction, 122–123
  learning results, 126–127

level of thinking, 123–124
quality of discussion, 118–124
questionnaires, 119
records, 127
results, 112
rubrics, 111–112
setting the stage and, 118
what to assess, 110–111
who will perform, 111

B

background knowledge, 28–29, 59–62
background knowledge quiz activity, 60
Bahktin, 17
Billings, Laura, 75
boiling water activity, 46–47
Brel, J., *Old Folks*, 53–54
Burke, Carolyn, 41
Buzz Groups activity, 31
Byars, B., *Pinballs, The*, 11
Bybee, Rodger, 24, 42, 47, 58

C

clarification, 95–100
  focusing, 96
  shaping, 96–97
  student independence and, 97–100
classroom climate, 58–59
closed task, 10–11
Coerr, E., *Sadako and the Thousand Paper Cranes*, 82
collaborative talk, 13
Confidence Rating Form, 43–44
conflict, insights and, 24–25
Connect and Extend, 94–95
constructive talk, 13
Consult the Class activity, 72

content area discussions, 42–43
    See also arts; literature; mathematics; science,
        health; social studies
continuing thinking after discussion, mini-lesson, 102–103
controversial topics, discussing, 79
cumulative talk, 92
curriculum
    assessment, 110–111
    goals, 22–26
Cycles of Meaning (Pierce and Gilles), 15–18

D
Daniels, Harvey, 36
Day, Jeni, 11, 13, 36–38, 104–105
discussion leaders, 92
Discussion Planning Sheet, 83
Discussion Stiflers
    "Coming to the rescue," 93
    "Hurry up!" 42
    "Just go discuss," 36
    "Save me, teacher," 88
    "The teacher is right," 89
    "We can't talk about that," 79
discussion webs activity, 32–33
disputational talk, 92
Dynneson, Thomas, 48

E
Eeds, Maryann, 15, 35
engaging students, 28
exclusion brainstorming activity, 63
expectation outline activity, 64
exploratory talk, 93

F
facilitation, discussion, 85–92
    independence and, 91
    independent work and, 88
    inviting participation and, 89–90
    sample whole-class, 90–91
finding big ideas, mini-lesson, 125
Fishbowl activity, 51

Fitzgerald, Jill, 75
500 Hats of Bartholomew Cubbins, The (Seuss), 50
Focus Assessor activity, 121
Focus, purpose, and engagement, assessment, 120–122
focusing discussions, 96
follow-up, discussion, 67–68
friendships, small-group discussion and, 74
Fuhler, Carol, 35

G
Gamoran, Adam, 10
gender relationships, small-group discussion and, 75
Gilles, Carol, 12, 15, 38
Gipson, F., *Old Yeller*, 50
goals, curriculum, 22–26
Gross, Richard, 48
groups, grouping, 59
guidelines, developing, 83–84
Guthrie, John, 19

H
Harste, Jerome, 25, 41–42
Hatchet (Paulsen), 23, 25, 50

I
ideas, engagement with, ownership of, 19
inquiry, spirit of, 58
insights, conflict and, 24–25
interaction, assessment, 122–123
IRE pattern, 11, 58

J
journals, 82–83
    reflecting on reflection, 106–107
    reflection, 104–105
    response, 54–56

K
K-W-L strategy activity, 65

L
Langer, Judith, 87
Leal, Dorothy, 18

Lee, H., *To Kill a Mockingbird*, 50
Lemke, Jay, 45
L'Engle, M., *A Wrinkle in Time*, 51
level of thinking, assessment, 123–124
Lewis, C.S., *The Lion, the Witch, and the Wardrobe*, 50
Lion, the Witch, and the Wardrobe, The, (Lewis), 50
Listening In activities, 13, 34, 53, 73, 78, 111
List-Group-Label activity, 61
literature discussions, 48–51

M
McMahon, Susan, 15
Many, Joyce, 18
mathematics discussions, 51–52
Mercer, Neil, 92
Miller, Margery, 73
mini-lessons
    continuing thinking after discussion, 102–103
    finding big ideas, 125
    prioritizing for assessment, 115–116
    reflecting on reflection journals, 106–107
    shaping an idea, 98–99

N
Nystrand, Martin, 10

O
Ogle, Donna, 65
Old Folks, (Brel), 53–54
Old Yeller (Gipson), 50
open-ended discussion, 10–12
orchestrating discussion, 92–93
    Connect and Extend, 95
    guidelines for, 93–94

P
Paris, Scott, 18
participation, 20
    inviting, 89–90
    sample whole-class discussion, 90–91
Paulsen, G., *Hatchet*, 23, 25, 50
personality traits, small-group discussion and, 74–75
Peterson, Ralph, 15, 35

Pick Your Spot activity, 73
Pinballs, The (Byars), 11
planning chart, whole-class discussion, 66
points of view, awareness of, 29–30
positioning theory, 73–74
Powell, Janet, 24, 42, 47, 58
preparation, assessment, 118–120
    reading, 28–30
    writing, 30–32
prep questions, 78
prioritizing for assessment, mini-lesson, 115–116
procedural talk, 93
Professional Standards for Teaching Mathematics, 52
Putting It All Together activity, 81

Q
questions
    effective and ineffective, 23
    goal oriented, 22–26
    selecting for discussion, 77–79

R
Rawls, W., *Where the Red Fern Grows*, 50
reading
    following up, 34
    preparation, 28–30
reading ability, small-group discussion and, 76–77
record keeping, 127
recursive discussion, 12–13
reflecting on reflection journals, mini-lesson, 106–107
reflection journals, 104–105
response journals, 54–56
Richards, I. A., 18
Roll of Thunder, Hear My Cry (Taylor), 50
Rosenblatt, Louise, 50
rubrics, assessment, 111–112

S
Sadako and the Thousand Paper Cranes (Coerr), 82
Santayana, George, 48
scaffolding students, 85–87
science, health discussions, 44–47

semantic webbing
    clarification activity, 97
    organizing facts activity, 49
Seuss, Dr., *The 500 Hats of Bartholomew Cubbins*, 50
shaping an idea, mini-lesson, 98–99
shaping discussions, 96–97
Sheppard, Linda, 14
Short, Katherine, 41
"Sick" (Silverstein), 50
Silverstein, S., "Sick," 50
single-minded talk, 10
small-group discussion, 70–83
    background knowledge and, 80
    friendships and, 74
    gender relationships and, 75
    group size and, 73
    making meaning and, 70
    personality traits and, 74–75
    positioning theory and, 73–74
    reading ability and, 76–77
    selecting members for, 71–72
    strategy practice and, 71
    student responsibility and, 70–71
    writing as preparation for, 80–83
social interaction, 14–15
social studies discussions, 48
Sounder (Armstrong), 50

T
Talk Tokens, 91
Tally Master, 91–92
tape recording, 13
tapping understandings, guidelines for, 87–88
Taylor, M., *Roll of Thunder, Hear My Cry*, 50
Think Alouds, 94
thinking
    charts, 108
    discipline-specific, 25–26
    higher-level, 18–19
    level of, assessment, 124
    social interactions and, 14–15

time, 35–41
    allowing enough, 41
    preparation, reflection, follow-up and, 41
    rethinking and, 41
    scheduled discussion groups and, 41
    strategies and, 35–36
To Kill a Mockingbird (Lee), 50
Trowbridge, Leslie, 24, 42, 47, 58
trust, environment of, 58–59
Turner, Julianne, 18

U
U-Debate forum activity, 67

V
Van Allsburg, C., *The Wretched Stone*, 36–38
vocabulary, 29
    building, 62–63
Vygotsky, Lev, 86–87

W
Where the Red Fern Grows (Rawls), 50
whole-class discussions, 59–70
    background knowledge and, 59–62
    follow-up and, 67–68
    how to discuss, 68–70
    planning chart, 66
    purpose setting and, 63–67
    vocabulary building and, 62–63
    what to discuss, 68–69
whole-class mini-lessons, 102–103
Wiseman, Donna, 18
Wretched Stone, The (Van Allsburg), 36–38
Wrinkle in Time, A (L'Engle), 51
writing
    following up, 34
    preparation, 30–32
    preparing for small-group discussion and, 80–83